M000227646

COMMUNITY CHURCHES

Making Disciples in Urban Areas

By Kelly Malone

Community Churches: Making Disciples in Urban Areas

Copyright © 2019 Kelly Malone.

All rights reserved. Except for brief quotations in critical publications or reviews, no part of this book may be reproduced in any manner without prior written permission from the publisher: Urban Loft Publishers, P. O. Box 6, Skyforest, CA 92385.

Urban Loft Publishers
P. O. Box 6
Skyforest, CA 92385
www.urbanloftpublishers.com

Senior Editors: Stephen Burris & Kendi Howells Douglas
Copy Editor: Marla Black
Graphics: Morgan Simms

All Scripture quotations, unless otherwise indicated, are taken from THE HOLY BIBLE, NEW AMERICAN STANDARD BIBLE ®, Copyright © 1960, 1962, 1963, 1968, 1971, 1972, 1973, 1975, 1977, 1995 by The Lockman Foundation. Used by permission.

ISBN-13: 978-1-949625-06-6

Made in the U.S.

Table of Contents

Illustrations

Acknowledgements

Community Churches: Making Disciples in Urban Areas is the result of learning to follow Christ with other Christ-followers in various churches. I am grateful for Christ-followers in First Baptist Church of Royse City, Calvary Baptist Church of Waco, and Stadium Drive Baptist Church of Fort Worth, who encouraged my spiritual growth during my early years in Texas. During my fifteen year sojourn in Japan, I both discipled and was discipled by believers at Wajiro Church in Fukuoka, Harugaoka (Spring Hill) Church in Kitakyushu, and Tokyo Baptist Church and Myogadani Christ Church in Tokyo. Since returning to the United States, I have continued to mature through the shared ministry of First Baptist Church, Bolivar, Missouri. For all of those who have followed Christ with me in these churches, I give thanks.

I am also grateful for my dean Rodney Reaves of the Redford College of Theology and Ministry, fellow faculty members in the Department of Ministry: Mike Fuhrman, Duke Jones and Prosperly Lyngdoh, and many students that I have taught in class, shared a meal with, or talked together over a cup of coffee or a glass of iced tea. Our conversations have both stimulated and clarified my thinking on many issues contained in these chapters.

I am especially thankful for Stephen Burris and Kendi Howells Douglas, my editors at Urban Loft Publishers. Their patience and continual encouragement through a series of delays as I seemed to move from one crisis to another enabled me to see this project through to completion. *Community Churches* would not have become a reality without your support.

Daily encouragement from my wife, Molly, and two great children who have grown into incredible adults, Maggie and Kevin, made writing possible. Sharing university experiences with Maggie and Kevin has broadened my understanding of disciple-making among millennials. Many sections of part two on the Shape of Disciple-Making Churches reflect what I have learned through this process. Of course, any shortcomings are my own.

I conclude with a special word of thanks to Jack and Barbara Darley. They provided many foundational insights on making disciples in urban churches while we worked together planting Wajiro Baptist Church in Fukuoka, Japan. I could not have asked for better mentors. I dedicate this book to Jack and Barbara, giving thanks for their many years of faithful service in Japan.

Finally, I give thanks to the Lord, whose sustaining grace and guidance made the writing of *Community Churches* possible. To God be the Glory!

Kelly Malone, Ph.D.
Bolivar, Missouri, USA
March 29, 2019

Prologue
Three Transitions

I remember riding a train through Seoul, Korea at night. Scattered on every hillside, as far as my eyes could see, were crosses illuminated by red lights. All of these crosses represented the location of churches—some large, others small, but all of them contributing to the process of transforming the people of Seoul into followers of Jesus Christ.

At the time, I lived in Japan where there were relatively few churches, most tucked away unobtrusively on narrow winding streets in quiet neighborhoods. I remember thinking at the time, "What would it look like if there were enough churches to transform a Japanese city with the power of the Gospel? And, what would these disciple-making churches look like?" Almost a quarter of a century has passed since that night in Seoul. I have realized my questions did not arise as a sudden epiphany brought about by an instantaneous action of the Holy Spirit. No doubt, God *could* have done it that way, but in my case he didn't. Rather, it was through a series of three transitions in my life that the Lord enabled me to recognize the need for churches as disciple-making communities.

First Transition

I grew up in a small town in Texas where practically everyone was connected to a church, but not everyone was meaningfully related to a church. There were many church members, but not so many church attenders. And there were even less committed Christ-followers. Many people saw churches as a source of services—weddings, funerals, and counseling. Some people attended church for worship, Bible study and prayer. The occasional potluck dinner or ice cream fellowship made churches centers for social interaction. But there was little recognition of how any of these activities could change how we went about living in the real world. So the non-attenders who asked, "What's the use?" seemed to have a point. Those who attended church and those who didn't acted about the same. There was about the same level of misbehavior and family dysfunction. Very few people saw churches as communities of disciples, or even recognized the need for disciple-making communities.

My small town eventually became engulfed in the sprawling suburbia that is Dallas-Fort Worth. My hometown has roughly ten times the population it had thirty years ago. Local churches also have grown in both size and number. There are now thousands of people living in new subdivisions scattered around the old core of my hometown that are not connected to any church. One irony of urban life is that people crammed together in neighborhoods and apartment complexes tend live apart in a "state of intense loneliness" (Frazee, 2001, p. 33). As Randy Frazee writes,

> They have too many worlds to manage. There are too many sets of relationships that do not connect with each other but all require time to maintain. [They] simply do not have enough time and energy to invest in each world of relationships in order to extract a sense of belonging and meaning for their lives. (2001, p. 33)

How do small town churches that once had at least nominal connections with everyone in town transition to become suburban churches that can form me aningful connections with the disconnected people that have moved into their communities? And how can these connections be utilized to encourage people to become growing Christ-followers?

Second Transition

I moved to Japan, where almost everyone is connected to a Buddhist temple, but very few people are connected to a church. Churches operate on the margins of society. Japanese cities are teeming with people, but not very many of them know much about Jesus. Japanese people celebrate Christmas, but Christmas is about trees, presents and fried chicken. It seems strange to Americans, but it is a Japanese custom to eat fried chicken on Christmas Eve. It is so popular that people order their chicken weeks in advance, and then wait for hours on Christmas Eve to pick up their order. The church down the street holding Christmas Eve services sets half empty. It is agonizing to live in a place where chicken is more important than Jesus. Most Japanese people do have a vague idea that Christmas is somehow related to Christianity, but neither can they explain it in detail, nor do they care to understand. Christmas is a time for merrymaking and fun.

It was during this second transition that I had multiple opportunities to visit Seoul, Korea. Like so many others, I was faced with the difficult question, "Why are there so many Christ-followers in Korea, but so few in Japan?" The red-crossed churches on the Korean hillsides burned my already burdened soul for the lost Japanese. I asked, "How can we ever form enough churches to make disciples in every neighborhood in every city in Japan?"

Churches on the margins of societies dominated by other faiths must find ways to transform the core of their cities. The good news is that some people in these cities move away from traditional cultural settings to become more "receptive" to the Gospel. The bad news is that "overstimulation from so many competing truth claims" can cause them to shut "out unwanted influences" (McMahan, 2012, p. 5). "A traditional faith that grows out of homogeneous village and family values has difficulty confronting the pluralism and diversity of the city" (McMahan, 2012, p. 13). How can we develop social networks that will enable us to make disciples across the barriers of ethnicity, culture, social class, and religion? Is it possible to connect with people who are radically different than we are in order to *share* the Gospel *with them* (as opposed to only speaking *to them*) in the context of "ordinary life" (Roxburgh, 2011, p. 133)?

Third Transition

When I returned to the United States, I found that churches that previously stood at the core of urban culture have moved to the fringe. Church leaders are no longer looked up to as models for ethics and morality. Christ-followers are suspected of violating new social norms relating to marriage, family life, education and the environment. Christ-followers running for political office attempt to get elected *in spite of*, rather than *because of*, their faith commitments. Churches find it difficult to adapt to these new realities because they are trapped in structures that worked well in the mid-20th century, but have long since outlived their usefulness. The old order has passed away, but the new has not yet come. We are passing through a time that Bill Easum aptly labels, "a time radical discontinuity" resulting in "chaos" (Easum, 2000, pp. 46, 53).

Christmas in the United States looks increasingly like Christmas in Japan—more about fun and merry-making and less about Jesus. Even "Christ" in the word "Christmas" has become offensive. Employees in department stores and malls are instructed to say, "Happy Holidays," in order to avoid upsetting customers. Traditions based in Christian symbolism—such as lights, trees, candles, and angels—have lost their meaning. Nativities no longer have a place in the public square.

This is a reflection of North America's shift from a "truth-orientation" to more of a "spiritual-orientation," with greater emphasis placed on "personal transformation" (Roof, 1999, p. 185). As many self-proclaimed "Christians" flow with the mainstream of American culture, they become reluctant to take dogmatic stances on traditional Christian beliefs and values and are more open to the possibility that various religions and ideologies may be "equally true and good" (Roof, 1999, pp. 186-87). Salvation through faith in Jesus Christ has become less important than finding acceptance and emotional support in a community of like-minded people (Roof, 1999, pp. 189-90). The meaning of "community" itself is being redefined as "face-to-face relationships" are abandoned in favor of communication through social media (Van Gelder, 1998, pp. 42-43). People search for meaning in a world of "endless choices," "transient relationships," "personal spirituality" that does not recognize the need for "organized religion," and cultural clashes leading to "random violence" (Van Gelder, 1998, p. 37). How can marginalized Christ-followers live and speak the Gospel in ways that will enable those in the mainstream culture to commit to follow Jesus Christ? What does it look like to follow Christ in a culture where people no longer see the value of faith commitments? Is it possible for churches to lay aside their encumbering institutional structures in order to become more authentic disciple-making communities?

Community Churches

In response to these compelling issues, *Community Churches* lays out both the necessity for and the nature of churches that become disciple-making communities in urban areas. The first section of the book focuses on the need for these churches. Chapter one provides a biblical basis for churches as disciple-making communities. Scripture describes a community of faith that exists for the transformation of people, both inside and outside community. This is true in the case of both Israel, which is called to be a nation of priests (Ex. 19:6), and the church, which is sent to disciple the nations (Matt. 28:19). Chapter two explains historically why the staggering numerical growth of Christianity has not always included spiritual growth. In many cases, churches in world's city have made converts without making disciples. Chapter three emphasizes that disciple-making churches do not always have the same structure. Various types of churches can be utilized for effective disciple-making, depending on the size and make-up of the surrounding community. What is important is that the church is a good fit for the people it is attempting to reach. Some possible types include: downtown churches, inner-city churches, neighborhood churches, house churches, and cell churches. Chapter four introduces some common characteristics of disciple-making churches. Typically, there is loose affiliation at the fringe, but strong commitment in the core. People on the fringe carry baggage from their former way of life. Growing commitment to Jesus Christ is paralleled by growing commitment to the disciple-making community. As growing Christ-followers take on the character of Christ, they release the baggage brought with them from their former way of life.

The second part of *Community Churches* discusses six elements of disciple-making communities: church structure, the ministry of the Word, worship, fellowship, service, and community transformation. Every aspect of church life should contribute to disciple-making. Relationships form that allow committed Christ-followers to influence others to follow him. As people study and apply God's Word together, they encounter the living Christ who calls them to follow him. Through worship, God transforms those who interact with him. Fellowship takes place in caring community in which Christ-followers serve each other and hold one another accountable for spiritual growth. This leads to service which bears witness to the love of Christ outside the walls of the church. As Christ-followers infiltrate cities, they transform the places they live, work and play with the life of Christ who is present and at work among his people.

Community Churches is not primarily an academic treatise on the nature and purpose of the church. It is also not primarily an instruction manual on how to develop disciple-making communities. Rather, *Community Churches* is a call to action. It challenges us to leave behind both debilitating beliefs and ineffective strategies in order to form communities of Christ-followers who are committed to lay aside the burdens of the present world in order to walk with Jesus Christ in the power of the Holy Spirit.

Call to Action

- **What experiences have shaped your understanding of the church's role in making disciples?**
- **How does your church make disciples?**
- **What do you hope to gain from reading this book?**

Part One
The Case for Disciple-Making Communities in Urban Areas

From its humble beginnings in an out-of-the-way corner of the Roman Empire, Christianity has grown to become a global movement of people from many nations, cultures, and languages. Christianity began as and is now primarily an urban movement. Yet there are millions of people in the world's cities who do not follow Christ. Every church in a city has the potential to become a disciple-making community. Part One provides a biblical, historical, and practical basis for the process of developing followers of Jesus Christ.

Chapter One
A Biblical Basis for Disciple-Making Communities

People often say things like, "I am only accountable to God for my actions. I don't have to worry about what other people think." This kind of individualism is a characteristic of Western Christianity and, as result of Christian missions, can be found around the world. There are two problems with this type of individualism. First, it is impractical: it does not work. Christ-followers cannot effectively follow Christ as individuals. So we feel compelled to follow Christ together in communities. We gather as churches for worship, fellowship and mutual support. We study the Bible and pray together. We do these things together because the Holy Spirit encourages us to fellowship together (2 Cor. 13:13). Many of us have experienced what it is like to try to follow Christ alone and we know we can't do it. We need each other.

Second, the Bible portrays spiritual life lived in community. This is true whether we are thinking of the nation of Israel in the Old Testament or the church in the New Testament. God's people participate in what he is doing in history corporately as well as individually. They are both the "agent and instrument" through whom God works to establish his reign in history (Hunsberger, 1998, p. 101).

It is impossible, within the limitations of this work, to provide an exhaustive biblical treatment of disciple-making communities. This chapter is intended to provide the necessary biblical foundation upon which to build them. It begins with role of the community in carrying out Abraham's call to be a blessing to the nations in the Old Testament. A number of cities are highlighted as examples of both the success and failure of God's people to transform where they live. In the New Testament, Jesus cast a vision for disciple-making communities that transform their cities and the surrounding countryside with the power of the Gospel. Acts and the epistles describe communities that come together, albeit imperfectly, to fulfill Jesus' vision for making disciples. All of these examples are instructive for us as we attempt to develop disciple-making communities as well.

God's People and Cities in the Old Testament

In Genesis, Abraham departs Haran, seeking a better place (12:4-5). The writer of Hebrews tells us Abraham was seeking a city whose "architect and builder is God" (11:10). God called Abraham to become the founder of a new people (Gen. 12:2; 15:5) who exist "for the sake of the nations" (Wright, 2006, pp.

57, 65). Abraham in no way "merits" God's promises. Rather, God's promises move Abraham to faith and obedience (Wright, 2006, p. 206). The promise is God's unmerited act of grace, to which Abraham responds in faith. God's "universal blessing" is "released into history" because Abraham *acts* in obedience to God's command (Gen. 12:4; Wright, 2006, p. 201).

God chooses to call Abraham, but Abraham also must choose to obey God's call. God calls Israel "out of Egypt," but they must choose to act in obedience to his call (Cate, 1982, p. 106). Because Israel is chosen, they are expected to maintain "God's honor" through "obedient service" (Cate, 1982, p. 105). Moved by God's love, Israel is called to love God (Deut. 6:4-5), which has as its outward expression faithfulness to his commands (Deut. 13:34; Dyrness, 1977, pp. 163-64). Implicit in this response to God's call is repentance or "turning from one's own way" in order follow the Lord's way. This is *not* a "once-for-all turning to follow God." Rather, confession and repentance must take place each time people fail in following him (Lev. 5:5; Deut. 30:2; Ezek. 18:30; Dyrness, 1977, p. 163).

"Walking humbly with God" involves "solidarity" with one's community in a way that reflects the will and character of God (Micah 6:8; Dyrness, 1977, p. 125). While we tend to emphasize the individual's personal relationship with God, in the Old Testament we find God is glorified within a *community*,

Israel as the people of God (Dyrness, 1977, pp. 168-69). This community provides a context for personal moral decision-making. For example, the Ten Commandments are not given to individuals, but rather to the people of Israel as a whole. Within their community, the people learn to live out what it means to love God and to love one another. This includes not only eschewing idols in order to worship only the true God, but also abstaining from murder, adultery, false witness, and covetousness (Ex. 20:1-17; Deut. 5:1-21; Dyrness, 1977, pp. 177-80). God chooses Abraham's descendants from among the nations to be his special possession (Ex. 7:6). Peter picks up this term to describe the "Christian community as the new people of God" (1 Pet. 2:9-10; Cate, 1982, p. 103).

Blessing is not a promise; it is a calling. It is a role that Abraham and his descendants are called to live out among the nations. It is God's response to the curse which has come upon the descendants of Adam as a result of his disobedience (Gen. 3). It is only possible to be a blessing to others when the people of Israel live in a "loving, trusting and obedient relationship with their God" (Deut. 30; Wright, 2006, p. 215). Only one descendant of Abraham, Jesus Christ, who is perfectly obedient to God, fulfills Abraham's call to be a blessing to the descendants of Adam (Rom. 5:19). The story of Israel is the history of how "God's blessing" comes to supersede "human fallen-ness" (Wright, 2006, pp. 211-13).

Cities play a crucial role in this story. Lot, Abraham's nephew, settles in the sin-filled cities of Sodom and Gomorrah (Gen. 13:10-12). The Lord responds to the "outcry of oppression" in these cities (Gen. 13:13; 18:20-21). Their men are characterized by "violent sexual immorality" (Gen. 19:4; Wright, 2006, pp. 272, 359). Abraham "haggles" with God, trying to save the cities from destruction for the sake of a few righteous men (Gen. 18:23-32; Wright, 2006, p. 361). This story reminds us that, at times, entire cities may come under God's judgment. However, even a few righteous people may bring about the preservation of a city. When we are willing to share "honest relationships" with "broken people," it is possible to bring about spiritual transformation, both theirs and ours (Smith, 2008, pp. 19-26). It seems that Lot did not always use his potential influence for good. For example, Lot offers his own daughters to the men of Sodom who want to sexually violate his angelic guests, and only the intervention of the guests preserves their lives (Gen. 19:5-11). Sodom and Gomorrah are destroyed, but Lot and his daughters are spared (Gen. 19:24-30). We can only wonder what would have happened if Lot had taken a more courageous stand for righteousness and morality in Sodom. While we are quick to judge, how often do we follow Lot's example: only trying to preserve the well-being of our families while we allow the surrounding city to go to ruin?

Nineveh repents in response to Jonah's preaching (Jon. 3:1-10). Jonah proclaims the imminence of God's judgment, yet it is contingent based on the response of the city's people. This is because he is a "gracious and compassionate God, slow to anger and abundant in lovingkindness" (Jon. 4:2; Cate, 1982, p. 79). God's love and mercy extend beyond the people of Israel to foreign cities as well (Hays, 2010, p. 301). Daniel Hays notes,

> The repentance of the Ninevites stands in stark contrast to the obstinacy of the Israelites. . . . Jeremiah preaches in Jerusalem for decades and response is only one of hostility. No one repents, from the greatest to the least of them. Jonah, by contrast, preaches a short, reluctant sermon in Nineveh (of all places!) and the entire city repents. (2010, p. 71)

Nineveh's repentance is "short-lived," so God uses the surrounding nations to bring about their destruction. Then "all who hear" the news "clap their hands" (Nahum 3:19; Hays, 2010, pp. 320-22). Repentance is not a once-and-done deal. A city that is preserved because it seeks the Lord one day may come under his judgment the next. Only a continuity of prayer, repentance and seeking the ways of the Lord guarantees the continuation of a city.

Babylon (2 Kgs. 25:1-13; Dan. 1:1-3) is both an instrument and a recipient of God's judgment. God uses Babylon as his instrument to judge Jerusalem and Judah (Wright, 2006, pp. 86-87). Yet even in Babylon, it is possible to experience God's blessing and "shalom" (Wright, 2006, p. 100). Bel and Nebo, the gods of the Babylonians, become a burden for those who seek their assistance (Isa. 46:1-2; Wright, 2006, p. 150), but God does not leave his people in Babylon to bear the city's humiliation. Rather, he promises to hear to their prayers (Jer. 29:11-14). Israel sees God's mighty hand at work, bringing protection (Dan. 1:7-21; 3:1-30; 6:1-23) and eventually freedom (Ezra 1:1-4).

Jerusalem is the holy city. During the time of Abraham, it is the dwelling place of King Melchizedek, the priest of the "Most High God" (Gen. 14:18). When Abraham offers a tenth of what he has taken in battle, Melchizedek blesses him (Gen. 14:19-20; Heb. 7:1-2). For the writer of Hebrews, Melchizedek represents an eternal priesthood whose likeness is fulfilled in Jesus Christ (7:11).

When David takes Jerusalem from the Jebusites, he does so using limited troops (2 Sam. 5:6-8), with minimal loss of life or displacement among the original population so that during the initial years of David's rule, Jerusalem remains primarily a Jebusite city (Bright, 1981, 200). David establishes a multi-cultural, multi-religious city as the capitol of his nation. Not satisfied with Jerusalem's new political status, David seeks to establish it as the spiritual center of Israel by moving the Ark of the Covenant there (2 Sam. 6). This is an attempt to displace the old Canaanite gods in order to re-establish Jerusalem as the city of the Most High God. The construction of the Temple coalesces Jerusalem as the central place for God's worship. This results in the close connection between the people of Israel and the city of Jerusalem (Bright, 1981, pp. 200-01) that has continued to the present day.

Because of the people's disobedience to the covenant, God turns against Jerusalem, allowing it to be destroyed (Ezek. 5:5-8). "With the Lord on their side, Jerusalem could not be destroyed. With the Lord against them, Jerusalem could not be defended" (Wright, 2006, p. 96). God's response to Jerusalem shows that while he is "sovereign over all nations," he plays no favorites. Even God's "chosen people" are not "immune" from his judgment (Wright, 2006, p. 96). The people of Jerusalem are unfaithful to their God, "prostituting themselves" to the gods of Egypt, Assyria, and Babylon (Ezek. 16:15-34) to the point of adopting their customs of child sacrifice (16:20-22;

Hays, 2010, p. 207). As was previously the case with Sodom, the Lord seeks a righteous man who will "stand in the gap" for Jerusalem, yet finds no one (Jer. 5:1-6; Ezek. 22:30; Hays, 2010, p. 213).

Judgment does not indicate that God is finished with Jerusalem: one day the Lord himself will enter the city bringing righteousness and salvation (Zech. 9:9; Wright, 2006, 119). Then the people of all nations will gather in Jerusalem to meet God (Isa. 2:1-4; Mic. 4:1-3; Wright, 2006, p. 339). "The temple of God" will become a "house of prayer" (Isa. 56:1-7), encompassing the "redeemed from every tribe, nation, people and language" (Wright, 2006, pp. 340, 347). God's "heavenly glory" which fills the "earthly temple" is a precursor of a time when the whole earth will display the fullness of God's glory (Isa. 6:3-4; Beale, 2004, p. 49).

Bethlehem is the least of the Judah's cities. Yet it is also the city of promise. While Jerusalem and the Temple are "left in a heap of ruins" (Mic. 3:12), Bethlehem becomes the birthplace of the Messiah, the descendant of King David, the Savior of the world (Mic. 5:2-5; Bright, 1981, p. 294). Bethlehem reminds us that no place is so insignificant that God cannot accomplish great works through its people. We often look to cities that are centers of commerce and culture, politics and religion, to produce world-changing leaders and movements. Yet transformation also may begin in small, unexpected corners of the globe. God does not need rich and influential people to change the world. Instead, he uses people who are willing to serve him. So he chooses a carpenter, born in Bethlehem and reared in Nazareth and twelve unknowns, mostly from backwater towns in rural Galilee, to begin the greatest movement the world has ever seen.

In the Old Testament, there is no instance of an entire city being transformed by the presence of God's people. Even Jerusalem is a mixture of those who are truly God's people and those who only ethnically identify with Israel. Whether in Jerusalem, Nineveh or Babylon, those who live in loving obedience to the Lord have a preserving influence. They are change agents through whom God works. Where their influence diminishes, destruction follows. Yet hope remains, because of God's unfailing love. Because of this love, God calls his people to become a community of blessing to the cities of all nations.

Jesus' Vision for Disciple-Making Communities

As Jesus travels through the cities and towns of Israel teaching, preaching, and healing, he feels "compassion" for people because of their "distress"—they are "like sheep without a shepherd" (Matt. 9:35-36). In response, Jesus tells his disciples, "The harvest is plentiful, but the workers are few. Therefore, beseech the Lord of the harvest to send out workers into his harvest" (Matt. 9:37-38; Luke 10:2). Other than his model prayer (Matt. 6:9-13; Luke 11:2-4), this is the "only other time in the Gospels when Jesus explicitly tells his disciples *what to pray*" (Wright, 2010, p. 258). While we use the model prayer regularly in both individual and corporate worship, why is this prayer used so little? Is it not, after all, a command of our Lord that we should pray this prayer? Perhaps the answer is *fear*. Perhaps we are afraid that if we pray this prayer we, like the first disciples, will become the answer to our own prayers (Matt. 10; Luke 10; Wright, 2010, p. 258).

The needs of the world's cities are too great to be met by any one person, even when that person is God's Son! While this may sound like heresy, the fact is that Jesus, confronted by the needs of the cities of his day, calls for reinforcements. Matthew places the setting apart of the twelve apostles within this context (10:1-4). And in both Matthew (10:5-14) and Luke (10:2-16), Jesus provides detailed instructions to his followers concerning their work: "Preach about the kingdom of heaven, heal the sick, cast out evil spirits, and even raise the dead. While you should not take worldly possessions with you, do not go from house to house like a beggar. Instead, find a benefactor (a "person of peace," Luke 10:6), who will support you during your time in the city. Use his house as a base for operations (Matt. 10:11; Luke 9:4). If the people of the city accept you, they have accepted me; if they reject you, they have rejected me as well" (Luke 10:16). The mission of Jesus' followers is an extension of Jesus' mission. They should rely on the Lord to meet their needs. And they should expect the same opposition he faced (Matt. 10:16; John 17:14-18; Kostenberger & O'Brien, 2001, p. 119).

While it is important to be biblical in the development of disciple-making communities, there has been a tendency by some to become *too literal* in their application of Luke 10 to contemporary disciple-making. For example, there is a strong emphasis on finding "persons of peace" (see for example: Garrison, 2004, pp. 211-13; Calfee, 2013, pp. 102-23). The "man of peace" is only mentioned in Luke 10:6, and no description is given. This provides little basis for missional strategy in the 21st century. Others would have us travel from city to city with only the clothes on our back, expecting the local people to feed and house us. This may work in some cultures that emphasize hospitality and have food and room to share. But what if we are in a setting where people have very meager means or where it is illegal to house foreign guests? In such circumstances, can we equate the refusal to entertain guests with rejection of the Gospel?

A more balanced approach is called for, such as the rules in Alan Roxburgh's book, *Missional: Joining God in the*

Neighborhood (2011, pp. 166-78). Some of his primary emphases are:

- Focus ministry on connecting with the lives of ordinary people in your community. Do not develop programs. Meet people where they are.
- Develop relationships, not strategies. Do this by focusing on sharing hospitality with others.
- Settle into the neighborhood. Become an insider. Live where you are called to serve rather than living in another place and traveling in.
- Eat *what* is set before you. Also, do your best to eat *how* the local people eat, even if it is uncomfortable. This communicates that you accept people and their culture.
- Help the people connect their personal stories with the bigger of story of God and what he is doing in the world through Jesus Christ. This is only possible when we *listen,* then converse about how the things of God converge with ordinary life.
- Encourage people to turn from old ways to new ways. Old ways protect people from running up against their anxieties and fears. Pursuing new ways gives God room to transform a community.

Focus on making small, incremental changes rather than trying to accomplish big things all at once.

Those Jesus sends out should work together, using a balanced approach in which both spiritual and physical needs are taken into account. As Charles Fielding, a missionary physician writes in his book, *Preach and Heal,*

> Jesus' practice of preaching and healing became the standard practice of the disciples. . . . Jesus sent out all of his disciples to preach and to heal. They were given one command, because the two ministries work together in God's master strategy. (2008, pp. 20, 21)

Jesus calls together communities of followers so that he can *send* them out to infiltrate cities and towns. His primary emphasis is sending, not gathering, and where gathering does take place, its purpose is so those gathered may be sent. This is the opposite of so much thinking about church and community in our day: we send in order to gather, and the goal is congregational growth. Many pastors have been taught to focus on the growth of their own congregations, often at the expense of working together with other churches to change their cities (Malone, 2016a, p. 116). In contrast, Jesus gathers his followers to participate in "reproductive spirituality." He trains them to be disciples in order to send them out to make disciples (Chute and Morgan, 2017, pp. 81-82). Reproductive disciple-making can lead to changed cities. As I have written previously in *City Church,*

> The *city church* must be about harnessing all of God's diverse resources within a city in order to transform the city for Christ. Individual congregations, with their diverse locations, sizes, places of influence, gifts, passions for ministry, leadership, and training, each have a crucial role to play in the transformation of their city. (Malone, 2016a, pp. 166-67)

Local congregations connected with one another through the "mutual interdependence" of Christ's body work together through witness and service to make disciples in their cities. This is not so much a structural unity as it is a unity brought about by the work of God's Spirit throughout the whole body. As congregations provide "fellowship, shared ministry, and mutual support" for one another (Guder, 1998a, pp. 260-64), disciple-making occurs on two fronts. Internally, Christ-followers within these churches are encouraged to move towards the "fullness of Christ" (Eph. 4:12). Externally, those who have been outside the community of faith turn to Christ and begin to follow him.

Disciple-Making Communities in the New Testament

Beginning on the day of Pentecost, a city-wide spiritual awakening occurs in Jerusalem in which 3,000 people turn to faith in Christ (Acts 2:41). This number soon increases to over 5,000 Christ-followers (Acts 4:4). This early city-wide movement is characterized by a strong sense of *community* as believers meet together, both "in the temple" and "house to house" (Acts 2:46) for fellowship, teaching and prayer (Acts 2:42). People sell houses and property and use the proceeds to help those in need (Acts 2:44-45; 4:32-35). A ministry team is formed to make certain that no widows are neglected in the daily distribution of food. Faith and the filling of the Holy Spirit are key attributes of the men who carry out this important role (Acts 6:1-5). But numerical and spiritual growth does not result in the conversion of the whole city. Instead, it sets off severe opposition. Peter and John are arrested and threatened with punishment if they continue to preach in the name of Christ (Acts 4:3-21). Then all of the apostles are arrested and threatened (Acts 5:18, 27). Finally, Stephen is stoned (Acts 6:8-

7:60). This expands to a "great persecution against the church in Jerusalem" (Acts 8:1).

As Christ-followers flee Jerusalem, they develop disciple-making communities in Samaria (Acts 8:5), Damascus (Acts 9:2), Caesarea (Acts 10), and Antioch (Acts 11:20-26). Later, under Paul's leadership, this Christ-movement expands further into Cyprus, Cilicia and Galatia (Acts 13), and then penetrates the great cities of Philippi (Acts 16), Thessalonica (Acts 17:1-9), Athens (Acts 17:15-34), Corinth (Acts 18:1-8), and Ephesus (Acts 18:19-19:41). Paul's strategy is to lay the foundation for "Christian community" in "regional centers" of "culture, commerce, politics, and religion." He hopes that "from these regional centers the gospel will be carried into the surrounding countryside and towns" (Bosch, 1991, p. 130). This expansion results in the issue of whether Gentile-background believers should be required to follow the Jewish Law in order to be recognized as members of the Christian community. An apostolic council meeting in Jerusalem decides that Gentiles can become Christ-followers without adherence to every aspect of the Law. However, they encourage Gentile believers to refrain from practices that are especially abhorrent to Jews (Acts 15:1-20). This decision opens the door for greater expansion of the Gospel while minimizing the future influence of Judaism on Christianity (Kostenberger & O'Brien, 2001, pp. 150-51).

Paul's letters provide further insight into the both the need for and means of disciple-making in some first-century churches. For example, Paul writes to a Corinthian church divided by factionalism (1 Cor. 1:12-13) and mired by idolatry and worldly living (1 Cor. 5:10-11; 6:9-10; 8:1-10:7). As a result of social class divisions, they violate the communal spirit of the Lord's Supper (1 Cor. 11:17-34). Only a few Christ-followers in Corinth are wealthy, while the vast majority live "below the level of subsistence and [depend] on communal meals for nourishment" (Welborn, 2016, p. 73). Providing care for the poor through "corporate meals" and the collection and distribution of food should have set apart the Christian community from other urban associations that tended to discriminate membership on the basis of economic status (Longenecker, 2009, pp. 52-53). But instead, the wealthy partake in "gluttony" and "drunkenness" while the poor go "hungry," to the point that many become sick and die due to the "failure of the Corinthians to discern the needs of members of the body of Christ" (1 Cor. 11:29-30; Welborn, 2016, pp. 66-67).

The key disciple-making principle in this epistle is stated 1 Corinthians 9:1: "Be imitators of me, just as I also am of Christ." On the one hand, this seems to be a bold assertion: that believers in Corinth need look no further than Paul in order to find a model of what it means to follow Christ. On the other hand, Paul is only stating the obvious: we learn to follow Christ through the example of others who follow him. Paul is not suggesting that each person should become an apostle. Rather, he is encouraging each person to live in a Christ-like manner, and to use his or her spiritual gifts to encourage others to follow Christ (Kostenberger & O'Brien, 2001, p. 196). Disciple-making is not, and never has been, merely a matter of knowledge we can learn by reading a book. It is, rather, a matter of what we do— how we live. We learn to live for Christ by following the example of others who live for him.

The primary outcome of spiritual maturation is Christ-like love for one another. Jesus said that we prove we are his disciples by bearing spiritual fruit (John 15:8). This "fruit" is the love of the Father and the Son in us (John 15:9); to "love one another" as Jesus has loved us: a sacrificial love that causes a person to "lay down his life for his friends" (John 15:12-13). This love is the "fruit" of the Spirit's work (Gal. 5:22) as we learn to keep in step with him (Gal. 5:25). As Grenz and Smith state so eloquently, "The Spirit provides the necessary power for godly lives," but "we have a role in the process. . . . He works through our cooperation" (2014, p. 162).

"Spiritual formation" leads to the "Spirit's fruit of patience, gentleness, [and] humility" which results in "oneness" among Christ-followers in Ephesus (Stroope, 2017, p. 377). They have "one Lord, one faith, one baptism, one God and Father of all who is over all and through all and in all" (4:5-6). This, in turn, leads to witness and transformation (Stroope, 2017, p. 399). This unity is not found in a single congregation, but rather in a "strong network among the house churches within the one city and those in other cities" (Martin, 2009, p. 117). Within this unified community, the Lord provides for service through equipping apostles, prophets, evangelists, pastors, and teachers (4:11). This five-fold pattern is not limited to leadership, but rather describes the whole church working together to build one another up (4:12) in order to achieve unity of faith, knowledge of God's Son, and spiritual maturity, which is measured by Christ-likeness (4:13, 15; Frost & Hirsch, 2003, pp. 168-72).

Katartismon, the word translated "prepare" (4:12), also can be translated "mend" or "restore," and can be used for "setting a broken bone." Both individual healing and corporate restoration are necessary prerequisites for spiritual growth (Hull, 1990, p. 163). What is most important is that spiritual maturity takes place as believers follow Christ together in community. "The Christian life is not merely an individual struggle for perfection" (Grenz & Smith, 2014, p. 183). It is a result of life lived in "harmony with each other as Christ-followers share in "values," "sympathy," "compassion," and "mission" together (Grenz & Smith, 2014, pp. 183, 184).

"Harmony" among Christ-followers extends beyond their community to "reconciling the world" (2 Cor. 5:19). God is "reconciling the world in Christ and through the body of Christ, the church" (Gorman, 2015, pp. 166-67). Those who follow Christ are expected to leave behind their former commitments to their own ethnicities, cultures and gods in order to take part in a "new, tightly bonded, exclusive community" (Meeks, 1983, p. 190; quoted in Martin, 2009, p. 118). This takes place when "peacemaking, harmony, self-giving love, and forgiveness" are "evidenced in *all* relationships in which believers participate" (cf. Eph. 4:31-5:2; Gorman, 2015, p. 185). As Christ-followers "infiltrate" their cities and neighborhoods with lives transformed by the Gospel, people "encounter Jesus from *within* their own cultures and from *within* their own communities" (Frost and Hirsch, 2003, pp. 40-41). As the church "cultivates communal practices that embody the grace and love of Jesus," it subverts the "corrupted and destructive patterns of life" in the world (Gombis, 2010, pp. 182-83; quoted in Gorman, 2015, p. 207). Those who have been "justified" through faith in Christ practice a "liberating justice" that "raises up the poor [and] needy" (Gorman, 2015, p. 230, 237). Disciple-making communities become "active agents of goodness, compassion, reconciliation, and justice" in an unjust world (Gorman, 2015, p. 255). This most often takes place, not through "supernatural" practices, but rather through "ordinary human behavior: joining and sharing, eating and drinking, listening and caring, testing and deciding, welcoming and befriending" (Dietterich, 1998, p. 181).

Sent Communities

From the Scriptures, it is clear that disciple-making should take place within communities. Jesus never sends individuals to make disciples. He sends at least two, but usually more than two (Matt. 10:5; Luke 9:1-2; 10:1; Acts 1:8). When we read the Great Commission (Matt. 28:16-20) through American eyes, we may get the impression that after the eleven apostles received Jesus' command they scattered one-by-one to make disciples of the nations. A quick reading of Acts clears away this misconception.

We see a community of apostles working together to equip thousands of new disciples in Jerusalem. These first disciples gather from house to house throughout Jerusalem for fellowship, pray, teaching, and worship (Acts 2:42-47). They learn together, in the context of community, what it means to follow Jesus. When these Christ-followers are compelled by persecution to leave Jerusalem (Acts 8:1), it is most likely that they scatter in twos and threes, perhaps in families or cohorts of friends, telling the story of Jesus wherever they go. As they return to their hometowns and cities, scattered from Mesopotamia across the Mediterranean basin, they form disciple-making communities. This would have never happened if these early Christ-followers only gather in small homes on hidden back streets for fear of their lives. Rather, they boldly follow Christ in the power of God's Spirit. Through the example of their lives, they influence family, friends, co-workers, and neighbors to become his followers as well.

Call to Action

- What sins do you need to turn from in order to become an effective disciple-maker?
- What would your life be like if you became an "imitator of Christ" (1 Cor. 9:1)?
- What are some pressing spiritual, social, and physical needs in your community?
- What role could your church play in meeting some of those needs?
- How can your church become a blessing to your community?

Chapter Two
Amazing Church Growth, but Limited Disciple-Making

In a little over two thousand years, Christianity has grown from a few Christ-followers huddled in an upper room in Jerusalem to become the largest spiritual movement in the world. There are now over two billion people in the world who consider themselves to be "Christians," and that number continues to increase daily, especially in Asia, Africa, and Latin America. However, staggering numerical growth has not always resulted in comparable spiritual growth. Often there are far more so-called "Christians" than there are real Christ-followers. Space does not allow for a detailed history of the Christian movement, so allow me to support this assertion by using four examples: the growth of Christianity under Augustine, the growth of Christianity in Europe, the advance of Christianity in the United States, and the recent multiplication of Christians in Africa, Asia and Latin America.

Constantine—Christianity Politicized

Rodney Stark estimates that from the end of the first century to the beginning of the fourth century, the number of Christians in the Roman Empire increased from a few thousand to over six million (1997, p. 6). There are a number of factors that account for this remarkable growth. Faith in Christ advanced through "social networks" as people shared the Gospel with family and friends (Stark, 1997, pp. 16-18). This occurred most often in growing Roman cities, which were multicultural and allowed for a broad range of "social deviancy." Christianity was only one among many experimental spiritual movements at the time (Stark, 1997, pp. 132-45). Many early converts came from "Hellenized Jews" and Gentile proselytes of Judaism who: had knowledge of the Septuagint, understood the Jewish component of Christian teaching, expected the coming Messiah, and would not have been put off by the concept of a crucified and risen Lord (Stark, 1997, pp. 61-65).

Between A.D. 300 and 350, the number of Christians in the Roman Empire suddenly increased from just over six million to almost 34 million (Stark, 1997, p. 7). The most important factor in this upsurge was the altered political status of Christianity under Emperor Constantine. Constantine first gave Christianity equal status with other religions in the empire (A.D. 311-324), then following the defeat of his last rival for emperor openly favored Christianity over other religions (A.D. 324-337) (Lynch, 2010, p. 125). Constantine was first devoted to the Roman sun god, *Sol Invictus,* but following his victory over Maxentius at the Milvian Bridge in 312, he began to equate this sun god with the Christian Son of God. For much of his life,

Constantine believed in the Christian God "without rejecting other gods." However, near the end of his life he may have become a committed Christian in that he received Christian baptism on his death bed (Lynch, 2010, pp. 127-29).

Constantine sought to make Christianity the "cement of the empire." So he personally presided over the Council of Nicea (A.D. 325) and exiled Arius for his refusal to submit to the Nicene Creed, but later allowed him to return when Arius agreed to compromise. The emperor's "main interest was political rather than theological": he sought to hold his empire together rather than to see it ruptured by theological controversy (Gonzalez, 1970, pp. 282-84). As the state-supported church sought to dominate culture, it became politically expedient to be considered "Christian." The Latin term *religio* means "bind together," and from the time of Constantine, Christianity rather than the pagan religions was expected to play this role within the empire. Christianity became the norm in the cities, while many of the *pagani,* or rural people, continued to follow their traditional religions.

In 380, Emperor Theodosius proclaimed that all persons under his rule should "embrace the name of Catholic Christians" (Mullin, 2008, pp. 55-56). He proclaimed Constantinople to be a Christian city when most of its residents were still pagans (Freeman, 2011, p. 38). Practically all citizens of the empire, with the exception of persecuted Jewish and later Muslim minorities, became recognized as Christians, whether or not they were actually believers (Pierson, 2009, p. 58). Recognition of the need for faith in Christ and disciple-making diminished. In its place developed a church "run by a very worldly, political, luxury-loving, and sometimes notoriously immoral hierarchy" (Stark, 2003, p. 35).

Under social pressure, a "number of Roman customs" were absorbed into "Christian practice." For example, the "cult of the dead" in Roman culture developed into the "cult of the saints" within the church (McGrath, 2013, pp. 44-46). Ceremonies such as processionals and the burning of incense worked their way into Christian liturgy. The celebration of *Natalis Solis Invicti,* on December 25, a festival honoring the sun god, worked its way into the Christian calendar as Christmas, honoring the birth of God's Son. And the Lord's Day, the first day of each week, continued to bear the name of the sun (Mullin, 2008, pp. 57-58). The use of icons and images, strongly opposed among early Christ-followers based on the commandment against the use of "graven images" (Ex. 20:4; Deut. 5:8), became a means of grace, the "veneration" of which brought a person to an understanding the divine (Gonzalez, 1971, p. 200; Mullin, 2008, p. 79).

Europe—Christianity Paganized

Christianity in Europe continued to follow the Christendom model developed under Constantine. This was an urban-centered movement. Christians were divided into parishes led by bishops who lived in cities. Cathedrals were built as symbols of the church's centrality in urban life (Crawley, 1984, p. 41). "Christians in rural or small-town areas were considered as a part of the parish that was centered in the city" (Crawley, 1984, p. 39).

When Augustine of Canterbury convinced King Ethelbert of England to convert to Christianity, all of the people in his kingdom converted as well. Rather than tearing down old pagan temples, Augustine had them "consecrated with holy water" and rededicated to the "worship of the one true God" (Sanneh, 2008, p. 45). The result was numerous nominal Christians who maintained a thin veneer of Christian practice on top of deeply imbedded paganism (Marty, 2009, p. 87). For example, the pope took the title of *pontifex,* a title once claimed by Roman emperors as the chief priest of Roman polytheism. Easter, now the celebration of the resurrection of Jesus Christ, "bears the name of a pagan spring goddess" (Jenkins, 2007, p. 128). The building of altars over the remains of heroes was a common practice in the Middle East and the Mediterranean World centuries before Christ. Christians took this form to honor their own saints and martyrs. Furthermore, Christian churches were often built on the former sites of pagan shrines, and their relics revered there were "converted" to Christian use. This led to the development of pilgrimages to these sites in order to receive spiritual blessings, another custom with pagan origins (Freeman, 2011, pp. 9-10). Furthermore, "incantations and spells," leftover aspects of traditional spiritism in Europe, though not officially approved by church leadership, became incorporated into the everyday practices of many people (Stark, 2003, pp. 230-32). Later, these forms of "Christianity" were exported to Latin America, Africa, and Asia, where they readily mixed with the spiritual practices of traditional religions (Jenkins, 2007, pp. 128-30).

Of course, there have been significant instances of authentic Christian spiritual awakening in Europe as well. The monastic movement focused on the development of communities for mutual spiritual encouragement. This triggered Catholic mission work that resulted in the Christianization of Ireland, as well as the spreading of Catholic Christianity to Latin America, Africa, and Asia. In the sixteenth century, the Protestant Reformation brought about a renewed emphasis on salvation by grace through faith (Eph. 2:8). Beginning in the eighteenth century, Great Awakenings in Great Britain and North America resulted in spiritual conversion and disciple-making on a grand scale. This provided a foundation for the modern missionary movement, which began in the nineteenth century and has continued to the present.

The vast majority of citizens of European nations, with the exception of their Jewish and Muslim minorities, consider themselves to be "Christian." In 2005, there were 530 million of these Christians in Europe (Jenkins, 2007, pp. 2-3). Yet Douglas Jacobsen notes, "Only about a quarter of the population in Western Europe is religiously active, another half has some kind of minimal connection with organized Christianity, and about a quarter are self-consciously nonreligious" (2011, p. 132). There is a widespread trend towards secularism, less church-going, and disbelief in God (Jacobsen, 2011, pp. 132-34). This has pushed Christianity to the "periphery of city life" so that the "cities of Europe are a mission field again" (Crawley, 1984, p. 42). Since churches in this region are often state-supported, they tend to be seen as government services rather than communities of faith (Jacobsen, 2011, pp. 146-49). Christianity in Eastern Europe experienced persecution under Communism, but since the end of Communist rule there has been a resurgence among Orthodox, Catholic and evangelical churches. Still, in most of these countries only 10 to 15 percent of the population are actively involved in churches. And many young people have difficulty believing that God is real (Jacobsen, 2011, pp. 92-93).

Millions of people from Asia and Africa have migrated to Europe, with the vast majority settling in the cities. While many of these immigrants are Muslims and Hindus, many are also Christians. Among them are thousands of Christ-followers from Asia, Africa, and the Americas who are attempting to reconvert Europe. Or, it might be argued, they are attempting to bring about a wide-spread movement of Christian disciple-making in Europe for the first time. Many new disciple-making communities in the cities of Europe have an international feel. For example, Kingsway International Christian Center, one of the largest congregations in metropolitan London, has a Nigerian pastor and a majority of members from Africa and Latin America (Jenkins, 2007, pp. 245-48). These non-Western Christ-followers often "show greater spiritual vitality and evangelistic zeal. In many cases, their prayer life is deeper and they expect God to work with power" (Pierson, 2009, p. 327). While this has been referred to as "missions-in-reverse," it is more a matter of people "from everywhere" going "somewhere" to live out their faith (Escobar, 2003, p. 162). What remains to be seen is whether the making of disciples in Europe can penetrate the core of nominally Christian European peoples.

United States—Christianity Marginalized

In 2000, 225 million people in the United States regarded themselves as "Christian." This number is expected to increase to 330 million by 2050 (Jenkins, 2007, p. 104). Most of this increase is due to immigration. Over 60 percent of recent immigrants to the United States are Christian, compared with only about 10 percent Muslim. The largest number are Roman Catholics from Latin America, although there are also large numbers of evangelicals from Asia and Africa. Two-thirds of Chinese-Americans attend Chinese churches, and Korean Christians outnumber Korean Buddhists by twenty to one. Contrary to popular perception, about three-fourths of Arab-Americans are also Christians (Jenkins, 2007, pp. 118-23). In spite of Christianity's continued growth in the United States, it no longer forms the main stream of American culture. Americans are religious "freelancers" who choose faith and church involvement on the basis of personal preference (Jacobsen, 2011, p. 227). Most new congregations and new believers come from minority communities. And spiritual conversion struggles to address the key issue of moral transformation.

In the nineteenth century, in New England "moral reform" emphasized a balance between "human freedom and divine justice." In the South and West, evangelical revival aimed at converting the lost. While the New England movement was more intellectual, the evangelical revival was more emotional (Mullin, 2008, p. 182). The influence of evangelicalism in the United States might have been even greater had it not been for the issue of slavery, which divided most American denominations by the 1840s, and eventually led to Civil War (Mullin, 2008, pp. 192-93). Unfortunately, Christian conversion did not necessarily lead to a greater sense of social justice. In 1832, when Frederick Douglass heard that his master had experienced conversion, Douglass hoped that his master would either emancipate his slaves or at least treat them more humanely. He did neither. Douglass writes, "I believe him to have been a much worse man after his conversion than before" (Meachum, 2007, p. 125). Those who claim conversion do not always experience moral transformation. Meachum concludes that America is only a "Christian nation . . . in the sense that it [i]s a nation populated by people who identif[y] themselves as Christians" (2007, p. 144).

From the mid-20th century, mainline Protestant churches have lost almost fifty percent of their members (Jacobsen, 2011, p. 233). In contrast, American evangelicalism has come into international prominence. It is not only about "saving America," but also reaching the world for Christ (Shaw, 2010, pp. 116, 119). Unfortunately, evangelicalism is often linked with middle-class values that overlook the need for economic equality and social justice (Shaw, 2010, p. 126). As faith has become "personalized," society has become "individualized," and morality has become "relativized" (Van Gelder, 1998, pp. 54-55). As a result, churches often fail to form disciple-making communities that transform their cities for Christ.

Middle-class culture prefers "privacy, possessions, and power" and dislikes "poverty, weakness, and dependency" (Ellison, 1997, p. 99). Sometimes there is a tendency to focus on spiritual needs to the exclusion of physical and social needs (pp. 99-100). Churches often focus on meeting the needs of their own members rather than reaching their communities (Jacobsen, 2011, pp. 234-35). The result is churches filled with activity that suffer from a lack of "genuine spiritual vitality." Members are encouraged to attend church, participate in worship and a small group, and use their spiritual gifts for ministry in the church. However, more often than not, the result is only "tired, burned-out members" rather than spiritually mature Christ-followers (McNeal, 2003, pp. 7-8).

There is a tendency to "marginalize" newcomers as "invaders" to be treated with "suspicion" rather than "neighbors" to be served with Christ-like love (Looney, 2015, pp. 64-65). People are neighbors with people with whom they share common values, but often this "neighborliness [does] not cross the lines of ethnicity and social class" (Malone, 2016b, p. 82). In cities that are "patchwork quilts of ethnic, economic, and language groups" (Scanlon, 1984, p. 174), "churches may find themselves in communities that are geographically close, but culturally distant" (Malone, 2016b, p. 87). Ethnic, cultural, and religious pluralism in America's cities is making it a challenge to develop the relationships necessary for making disciples (Bakke, 1984, pp. 82-83). We must love those whose culture differs from our own with "intentionality, cultural sensitivity, and patience" (Looney, 2015, p. 183).

Asia, Africa and Latin America—Christianity Globalized

The recent globalization of Christianity is well documented. In 1950, "eighty percent of the world's Christians" lived in Europe and North America. In 2005, well over half of the world's Christians lived in Asia, Africa, and Latin America (Sanneh, 2008, p. xx), and by 2025, that statistic is expected to exceed eighty percent (Jenkins, 2007, p. 2). This is not so much because of the stagnation of Christianity in Europe and North America as it is the staggering growth of the number of Christians in other areas of the world. In 1900, there were approximately ten million Christians in sub-Saharan Africa. By 2000, this number had reached 360 million (Jenkins, 2007, p. 4), and is projected to reach over 600 million by 2025 (p. 195).

In 1949, when missionaries were expelled, there were about three million Catholics and one million Protestants in China (Sanneh, 2008, 248). While it is difficult to get an exact count, in 2007, conservative estimates on the number Christians in China ranged from 50 to 75 million, of which about five million were Catholic (Stark & Wang, 2015, p.11). In roughly same period of time, the number of Christians in Korea has increased from 300,000 to over 12 million (Jenkins, 2007, p. 82). Latin America has long had a Christian identity. Beginning in the 20th century, there has been a decisive shift from Catholic to evangelical, most of whom are Charismatic. While the vast majority of the population is still Catholic, evangelicals now account for over ten percent, and in some nations much more than that. In Guatemala, the statistic is almost thirty percent. All told, of about 500 million Christians in Latin America over fifty million are evangelicals (Jacobsen, 2011, p. 207).

About the same time that Christianity globalized, the globe urbanized. In 1800, London was the only city in the world that exceeded one million in population. Now, there are perhaps five hundred cities of this size. There are over twenty metropolitan areas with populations exceeding ten million. The largest of these, Tokyo, has about 38 million people ("Top 20 Megacities"). In the developing world, people are lured to the city by the possibility of "better education, healthcare, and economic possibilities." Unfortunately, "most end up in the growing slums" (Pierson, 2009, p. 344). People who move to the city seeking a better life are more open to change, including spiritual change. Separated from the spiritual traditions of their former ways of life, they seek a new beginning. So when they hear Good News about new life through faith in Jesus Christ, they are likely to believe in him. Churches have the opportunity to become "welcoming communities" to the newcomers, both to the city and to the faith (Pierson, 2009, p. 346).

Once again, space limitations do not allow for an exhaustive treatment of the recent global expansion of Christianity, particularly as it pertains to the world's cities. So I will provide only one example each from Asia, Africa, and Latin America: urban Christianity in China, some examples of African Initiated Churches, and Charismatic Christianity in Brazil.

Urban Christianity in China

Since the 1940s, the status of Christianity in China has moved from "ghetto" towards "mainstream." This does not mean that all persecution of Christians has ceased. However, in some cases house-church Christians, once an imprisoned and persecuted minority, are treated as "productive citizens" (Shaw, 2010, p. 196). The number of Christians in China now outnumbers the number of Communist party members, and if the present growth rate continues, the number of Christians in

China could exceed 500 million by mid-century (Stark & Wang, 2015, pp. 113-15). In this case, the number of Christians in China would exceed the population of the United States, and China could become the pre-eminent Christian nation on earth. As in other nations, many Chinese are turning to faith in Christ because they see it as a source of "hope, meaning, and forgiveness and church participation supplies a supportive social network" (Stark & Wang, 2015, p. 119). There are even incidences of Communist Party members attending church and becoming "secret Christians" (Stark & Wang, 2015, pp. 125-26).

Until recently, in China it was far more likely for people in rural areas than cities to be Christians. Over 90 percent of these rural Christians have come to faith in Christ through the influence of family members, friends or neighbors. In rural areas, Christianity often grows through "kinship networks" so that churches take the form of "extended family" (Stark & Wang, 2015, pp. 104-07). Chinese people who migrate from rural areas into the cities in search of economic prosperity discover a "free marketplace" of competing views regarding "lifestyle and belief" (Fulton, 2015, p. 17). In this environment, the churches in China's cities have begun to grow as well. Some of these churches are made up of "migrant factory workers" led by "migrant pastors" who moved to the city with them to work in the factories as well. However, other churches are comprised of middle-aged, university-trained professionals who have become disenchanted with the government and "their own inability to bring about social" change. They have become interested in Christianity as a possible source of personal and social transformation (Fulton, 2015, pp. 9-10).

Many of these new urban churches meet in rented facilities (rather than homes) and have full-time leaders (Fulton, 2015, p. 24). Many of these leaders receive formal theological training, either through Western theological schools or "Christian studies centers" that have sprung up at Chinese universities (Fulton, 2015, pp. 34-35). However, because of the lack of role models, some of these pastors fall back on Confucian authoritarian leadership models that are native to Chinese culture (Fulton, 2015, pp. 30-31). This results in one-way, top-down communication and inhibits the kind of mentorship needed for authentic disciple-making (Fulton, 2015, p. 33). Pastors complain of "Sunday Christians" who attend worship but "demonstrate scant evidence of a Christian commitment" (Fulton, 2015, p. 53). Due to an over concern about personal wellbeing, many Chinese Christians struggle to address issues such as marriage and family life, responding to the needs of others (such as the elderly), and social justice. Until these issues are addressed, Chinese churches will have limited impact as disciple-making communities in their cities (Fulton, 2015, pp. 53-66).

African Initiated Christianity

In the 19th century, some Christians in West Africa concluded that the old spiritual order of idol worship, divination, and spirit possession was dying away. "The white man's way of worshiping God was spreading and would one day prevail" (Sanneh, 2008, p. 186). Not content to follow the lead of white American and European missionaries who often disparaged African cultures, African leadership began to step forward, proclaiming a Gospel contextualized for Africans. Garrick Sokari Braide of Niger preached against the idols and amulets of traditional religions. He argued that the power of the Christian God was greater than the power of the old gods (Sanneh, 2008, p. 188). William Wade Harris of the Ivory Coast, eschewing the Western-style clothing of white colonialists, donned a white robe and turban, commonly worn by Muslim imams in West Africa during that time. He carried a Bible and a bamboo cross to symbolize his Christian witness. Like Braide, Harris preached the power of the Christian God to overcome the powers of the old "pagan shrines" (Jenkins, 2007, p. 58). Within eighteen months, under Harris' preaching 200,000 converted to faith in Christ (Sanneh, 2008, p. 194). Simon Kimbangu began preaching in the Belgian Congo during the 1920s.

Kimbangu emphasized God's power to heal. He also invoked the power of the ancestors as mediators between God and the people. A denomination based on Kimbangu's teachings and numbering 6 to 8 million members continues to thrive in West Africa (Jenkins, 2007, p. 59).

One reason for the rapid growth of these African Christian movements is their contrast to Western Christianity. For missionaries in Africa in the first half of the 20th century, Christianity was a doorway Western civilization. In contrast, African Initiated Christianity came without binding Western threads. It addressed spiritual issues that Western Christianity did not touch: the Africans preached against idolatry, witchcraft and Spiritism. They tended to favor cultural practices such as ancestral practices and polygyny (Sanneh, 2008, pp. 200-13). Lamin Sanneh comments that "Post-Western Christianity" has "instill[ed] hope and trust" in African people "in the face of overwhelming power and suffering" (Sanneh, 2008, p. 214). "Influential African prophets won followers by acknowledging the older spiritual powers and absorbing them within a new Christian synthesis" (Jenkins, 2007, pp. 144-45). As cities in Africa grow, Africanized churches spring up everywhere in schools, movie theaters, meeting halls, and conference rooms. The beliefs and practices of both Catholics and Protestant denominations in Africa have been influenced by these churches as well (Shaw, 2010, pp. 161-62).

In spite of many contextualized, rapidly growing churches in Africa, all is not well. In 1994, Rwanda claimed to be over 90 percent Christian. Hutu tribesmen used machetes to murder over 800,000 Tutsis. Almost all the killers were Christians, and sometimes clergymen were complicit in these murders as well (Jacobsen, 2011, p. 157). As we have seen in other places, in Africa conversion without disciple-making fails to bring moral transformation to people and their cultures. African Christians are split over the issue of the legitimacy of polygyny, with many churches not admitting men who have multiple wives. Churches struggle to deal constructively with issues such as marriage, family life, and sexuality. Providing for basic needs such as food, clothing and housing is also a concern (Jacobsen, 2011, pp. 167-68). Some of this economic distress results from globalization: African nations that face insurmountable debt are unable to address the needs of their poor (Mahiaini, 2003, p. 160). Effective disciple-making is only possible within this context by responding to physical, family and social needs as well. Samuel Escobar notes,

> The gospel not only infuses people with new
> life and gives them a capacity to work honestly

and save for a more ordered and comfortable
life, but it also transforms the social conscience,
so that believers gladly learn "to share with the
needy". (2003, p. 153)

As people learn to follow the model of Christ in ordinary life, Christian communities develop in which there is "discernable change" in social structures, economic climate, and family life (Engel & Dyrness, 2000, pp. 94-95).

Charismatic Christianity in Brazil

Brazil has more Catholics than any other country in the world (Jacobsen, 2011, p. 214). However, there are now over 25 million evangelicals in Brazil as well. Of this number, around eighteen million are Pentecostals (Shaw, 2010, p. 137). Over fifteen million are members of the Assemblies of God (Jenkins, 2007, p. 73). Brazilians have been drawn to Charismatic Christianity by a number of emphases that fit their culture such as spiritual warfare, supernatural healing, racial reconciliation, and the eradication of poverty (Shaw, 2010, pp. 138, 145). They believe "God intervenes directly in everyday life," and they expect their faith to yield "observable results in this world" (Jenkins, 2007, p. 91). These emphases have even worked their way into the lives of Brazilian Catholics who desire these experiences of power, health and prosperity as well. Outside of traditional church structures, many Catholics have become involved in evangelical-like "base communities," small groups that gather for fellowship, Bible study and prayer (Jacobsen, 2011, pp. 214-17).

Brazil has widespread social problems. Almost thirty percent of the population is teen-aged or younger (Jenkins, 2007, p. 107). Many of these live in poverty as either street children or with their families in the growing *favelas,* or "shantytowns," in megacities like Rio de Janeiro and Sao Paulo (Jenkins, 2007, p. 86). Drug and alcohol abuse as well as gang violence are increasing. This is an example of what Sam George refers to as a "terror-culture," in which young people embrace violence in response to economic, social and political instability. This is found especially in societies that have large number of "unemployed males between the ages of 15 and 30" (George, 2003, pp. 57, 59). Young boys may be lured into gang violence by "machismo and romance of guns," especially when they lack "positive role models" (p. 63). In response to this culture of death, churches must model a cause worthy to live for: young people have "worth and value" because they are "created in God's image" (p. 65).

As Brazilian cities have grown, hundreds of new churches have been established (Shaw, 2010, pp. 148-52). Some churches display a "willingness to go where the people are, into the slums of the cities, becoming part of the neighborhoods, being available when and where they are needed, praying with and for gang members, drug addicts, struggling single parents, and anyone else who needs help" (Jacobsen, 2011, p. 212). These "churches provide a social network" that is needed in rapidly changing urban culture (Jenkins, 2007, p. 88). Disciple-making includes not only prayer, Bible study and worship, but also practical training in family life, job skills, and personal and social ethics (Jenkins, 2007, p. 91).

The influence of secularism and materialism within churches is also growing. Numerical and financial growth may be seen as signs of God's blessing (Wilson, 2003, p. 178). One example is the Universal Church of the Kingdom of God, founded in 1977. By the 1990s, it claimed millions of members and owned a television station and a football team. It also has its own political party and carries out missions activities in over forty countries. All of this is financed through the offerings of members who are promised "prosperity and financial breakthrough" if they are faithful in their giving. They also are offered spiritual breakthroughs in areas such as demonic possession and witchcraft (Jenkins, 2007, pp. 74-75).

Samuel Escobar reminds us that where the Holy Spirit is truly at work, Jesus Christ is always glorified. When the Spirit is at work, there will not only be numerical growth but also spiritual growth. This spiritual growth will be reflected in growing faith, growing love and acceptance of one another, and growing "compassion for those in need" (Escobar, 2003, pp. 125-26). In Brazil there are many wonderful examples of disciple-making communities that bear this type of spiritual fruit, but there are many other churches that do not. There is a need for greater intentionality in developing communities that will transform the cities of Brazil for Christ.

Unfinished Task

In their paradigm shifting book, *Changing the Mind of Missions,* Engel and Dyrness write, "We have made many converts but few disciples." That is, we have made many Christians, perhaps even many believers in Christ, but too few "mature believers" (2000, p. 83). In response, they call for a renewed commitment to the Great Commission (Engel & Dyrness, 2000, p. 84). They believe this is best carried out by "dynamic communities" that are: sensitive to God's leadership, motivated by a vision for Christ's reign among various cultures, characterized by mutual sharing, and committed to partnership and collaboration with others (Engel & Dyrness, 2000, p. 89).

While there is much to commend the vision of Engel and Dyrness, the task is made more complex by the fact that this lack of disciple-making is not a recent issue. Rather, it is a 1700-year-old pattern, dating from at least the reign of Constantine.

It has been manifested in church history in both Europe and North America. And it is observable in contemporary Asia, Africa, and Latin America as well. There are no examples of perfect disciple-making communities, even in the New Testament. Few have done disciple-making well, and far more have failed miserably. Many have not even tried!

Some may reflect on these somber facts and ask: "What's the use? Why try to do something so few have accomplished?" To these questions, I have three responses:

1. *The Lord commands us to make disciples.* How can we claim to follow Christ if we lay aside one of his most basic commands.

2. *People were created to follow Christ.* People only find fulfillment in learning to walk with Jesus Christ. So in disciple-making, we address this most basic, but also most comprehensive of all human needs.

3. *Cities are transformed by disciple-making communities.* In the 21st century, the world is urbanizing. People move to cities in search of new life. This new life they seek is found through faith in Jesus Christ. The hope of the city is found in Christ.

Already, there are signs of hope in cities scattered around the world. There are disciple-making communities of various shapes and sizes springing up in both inner-city and suburban sprawl, in both uptown neighborhoods and downtown ghettos. They are providing opportunities for worship and fellowship, learning and service, love and support. These churches do not have any one structure, but rather follow a variety of patterns that fit their various communities. In the next chapter, we will consider a few of these potential patterns for disciple-making communities.

Call to Action

- What political and social issues hamper disciple-making in your city?
- What are some areas of ethical and moral compromise among Christians in your church and/or community?
- What are some dangers when numerical growth is not accompanied by spiritual growth?
- What can we learn from the rapid growth of Christianity in Asia, Africa, and Latin America?
- How can you work with Christ-followers of other ethnicities, languages and cultures to encourage one another to grow spiritually?

Chapter Three

Urban Disciple-Making Communities

A generation ago, in the United States "church" meant a group of Christians that met together on Sunday mornings in a designated building, usually also called a "church," with a steeple, pews, a pulpit, and an organ. This meeting almost always included preaching, singing hymns, prayers, and an offering. The church was led by a pastor, usually a man, and if it was big enough he was assisted by other staff. However, this configuration of church is waning and has been "replaced by multiple nontraditional forms" (Snyder 2016, p. 102-03). These forms vary from "megachurches" meeting in gargantuan buildings on one extreme to "micro-churches" meeting in houses on the other (Snyder, 2016, p. 104). In this setting, we should avoid trying to develop a "new standard." Rather, local groups of Christ-followers should be free to "find the form of church that best faithfully incarnates the gospel in their own contexts" (Snyder, 2016, p. 105). These forms will "demonstrate the gospel in ministry to the homeless, to young people, to the elderly, to prisoners, to the terminally ill, to an immigrant population" (Guder, 1998b, p. 239). They may meet in any location that allows them to carry out these ministries in their community: an apartment, a "storefront," a rented hall, or a traditional church building (Guder, 1998b, p. 239).

I have met people who are wedded to only one model of church: either house church, cell church, mega-church, neighborhood church, or some other pattern. They invariably make two claims about their model: it is *the biblical* model, and it will work *everywhere*. From their standpoint, it *must* work everywhere because it is the only model allowed by Scripture. They are committed to a "uniform methodology" which they believe "will work regardless of context." This approach circumvents the need for "reliance of God's Spirit" to work among people in unique ways in each context (Sparks, Soerens, & Friesen, 2014, pp. 62-63).

A dilemma happens when those who place their faith in one model find a city where their model doesn't work. First, they deny there is a problem because the model must work. Then they blame *people* for not implementing the model the right way. Finally, they try to *tweak* the model to fit the local culture. This is a step in the right direction, but it doesn't go far enough. They must be willing to try other models. They must realize that any structure that enables Christ-followers to demonstrate the "transforming power of the gospel" is biblical (Guder, 1998b, pp. 226-27). Howard Snyder writes, "Structures are useful to the extent they aid the church in its mission, but are manmade and culturally determined" (1975, p. 160).The Bible allows for "flexibility" in structure in order to develop patterns of community that meet the demands of the Gospel in the local culture (Snyder, 1975, pp. 124-25).

The challenge is to develop what Michael Frost and Alan Hirsch refer to as "culturally diverse, missional communities" (2003, p. x). We must grow churches that "incarnate the gospel within specific cultural context[s]" (Frost and Hirsch, 2003, p. xi). This brings about various forms of community that effectively make disciples among the people who live in their neighborhoods and cities. In a single city, there may be a wide variety of disciple-making communities: magnetic churches that attract people from a wide area, inner-city churches, niche churches that connect with particular communities, neighborhood churches, house churches, cell churches, multi-site churches, and network churches. While all of these types of churches share much in common, they each have distinctive characteristics which allow them to play particular roles in discipling their cities.

Types of Disciple-Making Communities

Types	Distinguishing Characteristics	Role in Discipling a City

Magnetic	Draws people(s) from wide area	Provide city-wide leadership and vision; able to connect with a variety of peoples
Inner-City	Focuses on needs of people(s) living in the heart of the city	Sustain struggling communities through shared resources
Niche	Focuses on a particular type of people, such as ethnicity, occupation, or interest group	People with common interest come together for mutual encouragement
Neighborhood	Builds community through making disciples in a particular area	Provides a spiritual center for neighborhood life
Micro	Builds spiritual family in a home or another intimate setting	Provides family life for isolated city-dwellers

Cell	A group of small groups banded together for shared leadership and disciple-making	Small groups share resources in order to encourage one another to grow spiritually
Multi-Site	Able to serve multiple peoples through ministering in multiple locations	Link related congregations together to encourage disciple-making in each community
Network	Churches working together to make disciples throughout a city or region	Allows for the strategic development of new disciple-making communities in unreached areas of a city

Magnetic Churches

Magnetic churches are popularly referred to as "mega-churches." These huge congregations, sometimes numbering over ten thousand in attendance, draw people from throughout a metropolitan area. As a result, they provide visibility to Christianity in their city that otherwise might be impossible. Unfortunately, this size also allows for the possibility that diverse peoples will worship together without really connecting with one another. Within the crowd, people may be tempted to only seek out others with similar "language, customs, culture and belief" with whom to bond. Growth is not always a sign of health. For example, "cancer and other diseases tell us that growth may signal serious illness" (Snyder & Runyon, 2002, p. 65). Some people may be drawn to megachurches simply to get lost in the crowd. A gap often develops between the number who profess faith in Christ and those who actually commit their lives to "costly discipleship." When this happens, "superficial adherents" rather than "serious disciples" may set the agenda for the church (p. 67).

In order to avoid this dilemma, magnetic churches must form smaller congregations within the larger church. These may be regional congregations made up of a number of small groups of people who live in one area of the city. Or they may be a group of small groups who share natural affinity with one another, such as university students or people who have similar occupations such as healthcare, business or information technology. This dynamic combination of small groups and mid-sized congregations allows fellowship, service and accountability to develop on a deeper level. Spiritual accountability through well-developed small groups and missional action through global involvement provides an opportunity for disciple-making through magnetic megachurches that is difficult to replicate in small congregations. The diversity of magnetic churches challenges people to "embrace the biblical principle" of "heterogeneity" which includes "unity in diversity, acceptance of others, and brotherly love" (Frost & Hirsch, 2003, p. 52). In this way, magnetic churches may enable Christ-followers to experience the global expansion of disciple-making (Matt. 28:19; Rev. 7:9) within a single congregation.

Magnetic churches may send out mission teams to share the Gospel and meet needs among diverse peoples, both within their cities and around the world. This has given rebirth to the paradigm of church-based missions, in which individual congregations play an increasing role in carrying out Jesus' mandate to disciple the nations (Matt. 28:16-20). Churches are not only calling out and financing their own missionaries. They are also providing training for those they send out and developing their own missional structures. While this is an exciting development, it is limited primarily to megachurches that can afford to finance their own mission personnel. This approach could be greatly expanded through the development of cooperative mission enterprises among churches throughout a city. Another potential issue is the perpetuation of the non-cooperative model of developing local churches around the world. One church sending out its own missionaries will tend to reproduce the model of single congregations carrying out their own ministries in other cities. These individual congregations cannot change their cities unless they learn to work in cooperation with other churches. However, large congregations can provide global vision for disciple-making for other churches in their cities. When these churches share their financial and training resources, they can take the lead in sending out networks of cross-cultural disciple-makers from churches throughout their cities.

Inner-City Churches

Inner-city churches connect people who live in the heart of the city. Some of these are ethnic congregations, especially African American and Latino. As inner-cities becomes more diverse, some of these congregations are becoming ethnically and socially diverse as well. It is now possible to worship in churches made up not only of African Americans and Latinos, but also Anglos and Asian Americans. This is made possible through the intentional inclusivity of every type of person in the community in the leadership and ministry of the church. This sends the message that diverse people are not only welcome, but also have a voice within the church. That all kinds of people, whether Black or White, Latino or Asian, banker or former felon, attorney or artist, may join together around the Lord in "accountable community" (Haah, 2014, pp. 98-99).

Inner-city churches wilt when they turn inward and focus on maintaining their historical forms and traditions. However, they become vibrant when they connect people through worship, fellowship, and service. Communication is an important key. They must be conversant with the local people and responsive to their actual needs: these may range from healthcare, childcare, and family support to counseling and crisis management. It is important to recognize that the poor, the middle class, and the wealthy all have needs. Frost and Hirsch share the story of a young couple that walked around their community pushing their newborn in a baby carriage. Of course, everyone stopped what they were doing to "coo at a new baby." This gave the couple many opportunities to make friends and to share their faith by "infiltrating a community" (2003, p. 57). Another key aspect of communication is what Craig Brown refers to as "gospeling": engaging people in conversations about Jesus. In East Nashville where Brown serves, these Gospel conversations occur in two ways: entering into conversation while caring out loving action in the community, and gathering neighborhood groups where deeper conversations can take place in an encouraging context (Brown, 2014, p. 69).

Another key issue for inner-city churches is their ability to develop *sustained community*. Can these churches continue to provide life-changing ministries in their neighborhoods that have dwindling financial and human resources? Based on the number of inner-city churches that have closed their doors in recent years, many suppose the answer to this question is "no." However, this is not necessarily the case. Those who live in the world's slums are often vilified as poor, backward, dysfunctional, and criminal. Yet "slum-dwellers" may use great creativity in developing alternative lifestyles that allow them to continue to live, even under the direst conditions. This includes the development of various expressions of community, both legitimate and aberrant, from extended families and economic cooperatives on the one extreme to street gangs on the other (McQuarrie, Fernandes & Shepard, 2013, pp. 318-46). Churches that are willing to reconsider their ministry model to better fit the people in their communities may not only survive, but also flourish. This involves developing local leaders and disciples who have a heart for those who live among them. It may also include leveraging resources from the larger body of Christ, both from the city and the global church.

Niche Churches

Niche churches attempt to connect particular types of people with one another. These may be ethnic congregations, such as Latino, Chinese, or Korean. They may be congregations made up of recent immigrants from Nigeria, Romania, Myanmar, or the Philippines. But they may also be churches made up of artists, healthcare professionals or business people. While niche churches may be limited in the scope of people they reach, they have the ability to draw people within their niche throughout the metropolitan area. This is possible due to relational networks of people who share common occupations and interests.

Often niche churches will meet around a point of common interest. They may come together in what Frost and Hirsch refer to as "proximity spaces" where both Christ-followers and those who do not follow him "can interact meaningfully with each other" (2003, p. 24). For example, a church of healthcare workers may meet at a location in the city's hospital district. An artist group may meet in an art gallery in the arts district. A Chinese congregation will have a meeting place in "Chinatown," while Russian immigrants may gather for worship in a community center in a neighborhood where many of them live.

"Significant relationships" can be developed through "shared projects" as varied as neighborhood cleanup, gardening, art, daycare, and job skills. As participants engage in prayer, Bible study, fellowship, and service within this context a faith community "emerges" that interacts meaningfully with its "host subculture" (Frost & Hirsch, 2003, pp. 25-27).

One type of niche church was Bare Bulb Coffee Shop in Warner Robins, Georgia. Bare Bulb was developed by the First Presbyterian Church in Warner Robbins as an attempt to create a space where both Christ-followers and those who do not follow him could come together for significant conversations. The shop began as a place where people could have conversations over "inexpensive food and drink." Over time, various connecting points developed—an art group, a health and fitness group, a reading hour with children, and "Light"—a worship gathering on Sunday evenings (MacMillan, 2014, pp. 106-16). As a result of sagging business, Bare Bulb Coffee closed after five and a half years in operation (Bare Bulb Coffee closes its doors, 2016). Perhaps one reason for this was the difficulty of developing leadership for ministry from among people who tended to self-identify as customers rather than as a congregation (MacMillan, 2014, p. 118). At some point, self-identity as the Body of Christ is necessary for ongoing effective disciple-making.

Another example of a niche church is the Sin Heng Taiwanese Presbyterian Church in Buenos Aires, Argentina. Originally formed in 1982 to reach immigrants from Taiwan, Sin Hang Church has become a multicultural church with worship services in three languages: Taiwanese, Mandarin, and Spanish. The multi-lingual nature of Sing Hang Church's worship reflects the cultural and linguistic transition of its community: while first generation immigrants were most comfortable conversing and worshipping in Taiwanese, the second generation tended to be tri-lingual (blending with both the larger Argentine and Chinese immigrant communities), and the third generation has Spanish as their first language. In order to connect with all of these people, as well as ministry among recent immigrants from both Taiwan and Mainland China, worship in three languages has become necessary. While these three congregations are one church under a common leadership team, each worship service develops a liturgical style that fits its culture. Particular emphasis is given to racial reconciliation, both between Chinese and Argentinians and between immigrants from Taiwan and Mainland China (MacKenzie, 2017, pp. 145-48).

Neighborhood Churches

Twenty years ago, church growth experts believed that most neighborhood churches would be gobbled up by megachurches. Now they are making a comeback. This is because neighborhood churches have the capability to do something magnetic churches do not do well—"integrating" people who live close to one another into "collaborative" communities (Sparks, Soerens, & Friesen, 2014, p. 47). This may deepen face-to-face relationships among people who rub shoulders every day at the supermarket, the coffee shop, the café, and the soccer game. These relationships that develop naturally over a cup of coffee or by watching Jimmy and Janie play soccer may be transformed into disciple-making clusters, but only when the questions that shape "real life" are taken up into the church's conversation (Roxburgh, 2011, pp. 23-25). This leads to relationships that bring about "healing and renewal" through "mercy, hospitality, kindness, [and] service" (Sparks, Soerens, & Friesen, 2014, p. 48).

Identification between church and neighborhood comes about when "life in the neighborhood is at the essence of church life" (Warnes, 2014, p. 134). Northland Village Church in northeast Los Angeles realized that it can be more effective to participate in already existing community events than to create additional church-sponsored events for the community. So they participated in the local harvest festival and summer movie nights, helped with neighborhood cleaning projects, and got involved in tutoring children in the local schools. Community involvement prevented church people from turning inward. Bridges built within the neighborhood allow people to cross over into the life of the church (Warnes, 2014, pp. 130-34).

Disciple-making in neighborhoods can begin by forming teams of people committed to neighborhood transformation. These team members learn to see their neighborhood through "God's eyes," perceiving how God is already present and at work in their community. They practice "radical neighborliness" by building connections with those who live around them. This may be as simple as going out for coffee or as complicated as hosting a block party. The point is to be recognized as and to recognize others as neighbors. This leads to the opportunity to "listen to neighborhood stories" in which people share the rich variety of neighborhood life. This includes information about where to shop, stories about local schools and athletic teams, and descriptions of personal and family life (Roxburgh, 2011, pp. 182-86). Conversations allow people to discern where they need to become involved in what God is doing. This does not guarantee success, especially in the beginning. But the more they listen and the more they try to do, the more effective they become (pp. 187-89).

Micro-Churches

House churches are small groups that gather for worship, fellowship and discipleship. This is a bit of a misnomer because every "house church" does not meet in a house. They sometimes meet in offices, restaurants and school rooms. Because of this locational factor, other names are sometimes used such as "organic" churches in Long Beach (Cole, 2005, p. 22) or "POUCH" churches in China (Garrison, 2004, p. 62). The organic model emphasizes developing healthy churches through natural reproduction "wherever life happens": vacant lots, parks, locker rooms, offices, and classrooms; even bars and strip clubs (Cole, 2005, pp. 23-24). Cole writes that macro-growth is made possible through micro-growth. We multiply churches by multiplying disciples, leaders and small groups (p. 98). When we "infuse" the smallest unit of the church with "life-giving DNA," we "influence" the whole body (p. 99). For Cole (2005), this DNA includes: **Divine truth** through Spirit-led application of the Scriptures, **Nurturing relationships** in the context of shared community, and **Apostolic mission** that focuses on making disciples (p. 115). POUCH churches emphasize: **Participative** Bible study and worship, **Obedience** to the Scriptures as the mark of authentic disciple-making, **Unpaid** bi-vocational church leadership, **Cells** of 10 to 20 believers meeting together, and **Homes or storefronts** as the most common meeting places. Not every church meets in a home, but every church does meet in a non-cost accessible location (Garrison, 2004, p. 315).

Three common characteristics stand out: simple structure, sense of family, and spiritual growth through application of God's Word. The New Testament assumes "face-to-face" communities in which everyone "greets one another" and "encourages one another." This implies small groups where everyone knows everyone else on a first-name basis. When name tags become necessary, the group has grown too large (Snyder & Runyon, 2002, pp. 65-66). Familial relationships are experienced when people are able to share "table fellowship" with one another. Sharing a meal together allows for the possibility of conversations between people of different ages, social classes, cultures, and nations that otherwise would not be possible (Simson, 1999, pp. 82-83). The goal of teaching in this setting is to move beyond mere knowledge to obedience to God's Word in order to bond in "relationship to Christ" and be "transformed into the image of Christ." This teaching is more likely to take the form of a "short talk" (rather than a formal sermon) followed by interactive conversation. This participatory style allows people to draw what they need from the discussion to meet their current needs for spiritual growth (Simson, 1999, pp. 83-84).

House church advocates are quick to point out that during the New Testament period, Christ-followers met together in homes. As a result, some believe this is the only biblical form of church. However, the more common view is that this is only one of many viable forms of church, and that it is especially effective in areas of the world where Christ-followers suffer persecution, such as China or the Middle East. In other parts of the world, house church participants are likely to participate in another form of church life, at least on an occasional basis. This is because most people need both a small group where they experience intimacy with Christ and his followers and a large worship gathering where they experience a greater sense of God's glory. It is only when the possibility of these large gatherings are eliminated by persecution that people turn exclusively to house church.

Because of their simple structure, it is possible to form a house church quickly, sometimes within only a few weeks. For example, Wolfgang Simson (1999) writes of the possibility of multiplication from one to 165,000 house churches in only 20 years (pp. 107-08). While this might be possible, it rarely happens. This is because the loose structure of many house churches enables them to unravel quickly. One thing house churches do exceedingly well is minister to the needs of broken people, but networks are needed to avoid their tendency to turn inward as these churches help the hurting (Snyder & Runyon, 2002, p. 69). So it is important for house churches to be bound together with one another, and possibly other churches, for mutual encouragement and support. It might be possible to develop a network made up of multiple house churches working in coordination with cell churches, neighborhood churches, and niche churches to make disciples in a city. At the conclusion of this chapter, I will expand upon this idea is disciple-making church networks.

Cell Churches

A cell church is one church made up of multiple small groups. Usually these small groups will gather as a single congregation for worship, or "celebration," once a week. The larger congregation provides leadership, training and a larger sense of community for those who participate in the cells. Small groups meet together weekly for fellowship, Bible study, prayer, and service. Most "church life" takes place within the cell groups that provide mutual support. Where there is a lack of genuine sharing, prayer, Bible study, and worship are not enough to maintain the vitality of a small group (Simson, 1999, p. 141).

A cell church may be megachurch, a neighborhood church, or a niche church. Due to its cell structure, it has the capability of penetrating neighborhoods all over the city with small disciple-making communities. In *Home Groups for Urban Cultures,* Mikel Neumann (1999) emphasizes that varieties of small groups may bring about both spiritual and numerical growth in different cultures. For example, in 1995 and 1996,

New Life Community Church in Chicago grew from 45 small groups and 850 in attendance to over 50 small groups and over 1,000 in attendance (p. 3). These small groups are led by a well-defined structure made up of group leaders, assistant leaders and apprentices that is designed to "free people to do ministry" (Neumann, 1999, pp. 72-73). New Life Community focuses on spiritual growth through mentoring and personal accountability (pp. 102-03).

Another example of cell church is New Life Fellowship, a rapidly growing megachurch in Mumbai, India. This city-wide church is composed of 25 zones, each with its own zone pastor. It is further divided into 250 worship centers made up of over 1,200 house groups, each led by trained lay leaders. There are also "250 full-time evangelists who minister on the streets of the city each day" (Neumann, 1999, pp. 6-7). In this Mumbai church, most biblical teaching takes place through sermons by pastors in zone-wide celebration services. Then discussion of the message takes place in small groups. The goal is to equip people to apply biblical teaching in real life situations (pp. 101-02).

One other example is ROSA Church in Moscow. One of the largest evangelical churches in the city, ROSA has over 1,000 members and over sixty-five small groups (Neumann, 1999, p. 17). While Bible study does take place in small groups, ROSA emphasizes discipleship through modeling: teaching prayer through praying together, or teaching evangelism by doing evangelism together (pp. 96-97).

Neumann (1999) notes that "caring" is a key integrating factor in each of these churches. In Chicago, much of this caring takes place through meeting one another's needs during the week between group meetings (pp. 136-37). In Mumbai, group leaders visit in the homes of all of their members each week. During these visits, they take time to eat together, to share needs and to pray together (pp. 142-43). In Moscow, people that participate in the same small group often live a great distance apart, so time spent together in conversation over tea and a meal leads to opportunities for "caring and prayer" (pp. 141-42).

A balance of congregational and cell group life is important for spiritual growth. While a single congregation may grow to include thousands of people, in reality this is a "whole network of smaller 'sub-congregations'" growing by multiplication through division (Snyder, 1977, pp. 122-23). On the one hand, when "Christian fellowship demonstrates the gospel" there will be a multiplication of small Christian communities where spiritual gifts are utilized to bring about disciple-making (pp. 125-27). Snyder (1977) also notes that through this proliferation of small groups, the official number of churches may remain unchanged while the ability of Christ-followers to penetrate and change neighborhoods and communities that make up a city may increase dramatically (p. 130). On the other hand, these small groups of believers must meet together periodically as larger congregations in order to experience fully what it means to be the "people of God." These congregational gatherings may take a variety of forms—megachurch worship, citywide rallies for evangelism, worship and teaching, concerts, and festivals. These large gatherings bear witness to the solidarity of Christ-followers in the midst of social fragmentation brought on by injustice and sin (Snyder, 1975, pp. 106-11).

Multisite Churches

Multisite churches are a relatively new form of church. A multi-site church is one church meeting at multiple locations. Sometimes these locations are in one city, but they also may be spread out in multiple cities. Often there is one lead pastor over the whole church, but each site may also have a site pastor to provide local leadership and pastoral care. These various pastors work together as a leadership team. This allows for the possibility of sharing spiritual gifts and abilities across sites, so that the various sites can support and encourage one another.

These churches make use of up-to-date technology. It is technology which makes multisite churches possible. In some cases, each site may have its own worship, choir and/or praise band for the music portion of the worship. Then the lead pastor's sermon is "piped in" from one location to the others. In other cases, preachers travel from one location to another so that each site has a "live" sermon. Whichever method is used, those who worship at each site recognize they are part of a larger movement. This may be what draws them: to be part of something that is bigger than any one community.

In 2014, there were over 8,000 multisite churches with over 5 million worshipers scattered across the United States (Stetzer, 2014). These churches vary widely. First Baptist Church in Bolivar, MO where I am a member has five worship services, worshipping in three styles, meeting at two locations (First Baptist Bolivar, 2018). Life Church, an Evangelical Covenant Church based in Oklahoma, by 2017 had 27 locations scattered across eight states (Life Church, 2018). Sometimes, a multisite approach is only a means to something else. The Village Church, a multisite church with five locations in the Dallas-Ft. Worth area, is transitioning to become a network of autonomous churches. They believe this will position them to grow the "kingdom of God in and around the Metroplex and to the ends of the earth" (The Village Church, 2018).

Multisite churches have the potential to develop shared vision that can impact a whole city or a broader area through the sharing of spiritual gifts, talents and resources. However, if control is too centralized, it may diminish each site's ability to penetrate its own community. Too much uniformity among the sites may lead to a one-size-fits-all approach to church life that brings about uniformity and the expense of contextualization. Some decision-making must remain in the hands of local leaders at each site to achieve maximum effectiveness. This allows individual sites to develop worship styles, ministries, and discipleship methods that meet local contexts.

Another potential issue is that multisite churches sometimes fail to develop community at local sites needed to deal with personal issues. Sometimes there is a lack of pastoral care in cases of sickness and family issues. People who show up at sites with a consumer mindset may struggle to invest themselves in the lives of others who worship with them so they really never connect with one another. As a result, reproduction of disciples and spiritual leaders is often limited. On the other hand, Stezter (2014) points out that multisite churches tend to:

- Reach more people than single site churches.
- Spread healthy churches to more diverse communities.
- Have more volunteers in service as a percentage than single site churches.

- Baptize more people than single site.
- Tend to activate people into ministry more than single site.

Networks of Churches

Networks of churches are formed when people scattered throughout a city come together around the Gospel. This may include niche churches, cell churches, multisite churches, or even a network of house churches. What is important is the development of connections in order to make disciples throughout a city. "Integration" of an "interdependent system" is more important than any of its individual parts (Simson, 1999, p. 144). Since small and medium-sized churches are most efficient at making disciples, rather than attempting to grow larger churches, we should be attempting to develop expanding "networks of smaller congregations" (Snyder & Runyon, 2002, p. 65). This will result in disciple-making communities in diverse neighborhoods coming together to form a "community of communities" that is "multicultural, multiethnic, geographically extensive, and organizationally diverse" (Guder, 1998a, p. 265).

Networks of smaller churches sometimes form in places where larger churches encounter greater government resistance. For example, Zhiqiu Xu (2017) writes about three networks of churches in urban China. Hangzhou Church began with the goal to become a megachurch. But after persecution from the local government, it reorganized into a network of twelve "branches," each with less than fifty participants. While the government continues to monitor church activities, the church has been able to carry out public evangelism campaigns and to train members for spiritual maturity and service. Training focuses on three elements: "clear calling, basic theological training, and mature spiritual life" (Xu, 2017, pp. 118-21). Zhuhai Church grew out of a vision to plant churches among migrant workers in an urban area. This has grown to a network of over thirty churches with over 3,000 members. The church encourages workplace evangelism by people who have vocational training in a variety of fields such as barbers, auto mechanics and massage therapists. Discipleship focuses primarily on evangelism training. Effectiveness is demonstrated when a person is able to lead others to faith in Christ (Xu, 2017, pp. 122-24). Xinyang Church has fifteen branches with over 12,000 active members spread throughout the city. The church has been allowed to engage in service to AIDS patients, orphans and single-parent families, and hospital patients. However, the local government has resisted the church's ministries to children and college students. While Xinyang Church has been forced to reduce Bible teaching among children, the college student ministry has grown to the point that students now have their own worship service. In order to reach their city, the members of Xinyang Church are encouraged to share the Gospel with at least one person each day. The church provides training for members not only in evangelism, but also in basic theology and other ministries (Xu, 2017, pp. 125-28).

In cities, churches sometimes come into conflict with one another. When this happens, it is important to remember that the Holy Spirit is in control. When we submit to the Spirit, he can blend together "differing shades of meaning" in various explanations of the Gospel to bring broader impact (Malone, 2016, p. 129). As networks of churches work together to make disciples, the Spirit produces Christ-like love throughout the city (p. 134). Churches can work together in a number of ways to make disciples in their cities. Historically, this has been seen in citywide movements for prayer, evangelism, and church planting (pp. 101-07). While each of these movements have a limited impact, they have not gone far enough in bringing transformation to cities. It is possible to develop networks of churches that can help one another through shared leadership, resources, evangelism, and ministries. This may take many forms: a team of leaders with varied gifts from small churches who work together to strengthen all of their churches; large congregations helping to meet the financial needs of struggling congregations positioned in strategic neighborhoods; providing ongoing training and mentoring for gifted evangelists in churches throughout the city; and, churches working together to carry out strategic human needs ministries such as clothes closets, food pantries, soup kitchens, counseling centers, and after-school programs (Malone, 2016, pp. 117-30). The key is to develop a "community of believers" throughout a city brought together by common values of "grace, love, and fellowship" (p. 130). Working together as a network of churches both flows out of and strengthens these values.

Cities consist of various cultures, ethnicities, languages, and social classes configured into a variety of neighborhoods and networks. No one church will connect with all of them. So a variety of churches is needed to disciple this variety of peoples. In one city we should expect to find both megachurches and micro-churches, both niche churches and neighborhood churches, both inner-city churches and suburban churches. Each of these churches has a distinct role to play in making disciples. While these churches have both strengths and weaknesses, they all can become effective disciple-making communities.

Call to Action

- Which type of church described in this chapter best describes your church?
- What other types of churches are present in your city?
- How does your church make disciples?
- How do the churches in your city network with one another?
- What barriers prevent churches in your city from working together?

Chapter Four
Developing Disciple-Making Communities

Connecting with Jesus and His People

Reproducing discipleship, or making disciples who make disciples, is at the very heart of the Gospel. In Matthew 28:18-20, Jesus commands his followers to make followers. They are to carry out this command by teaching others to obey everything Christ has commanded (Matt. 28:20). In Acts 1:8, Jesus tells the disciples they will become *his witnesses*, proclaiming the truth about him in order to call other people to follow him.

Many kinds of churches, both large and small, inner-city and suburban, multiethnic and multisite, contribute to making disciples in their cities. The process through which these various churches become disciple-making communities is remarkably similar. They form relationships with people to help them develop relationships with Jesus Christ. The point is to "invite everyone to take their next step towards Jesus" (Harrington & Absalom, 2016, p. 45). This occurs through increasing connectivity: people connect with people who are connected with Jesus. Through these connections, those connected with Jesus invite those who are not yet connected with Jesus to seek him. Through seeking Jesus together, those who are not connected with Jesus before become connected with him. These connections may be loose in the beginning, but over time they become firmly established so that those who once had no connection with Christ are able to encourage others to seek him as well.

The development of disciples seldom occurs instantaneously. We must begin with people where they are and teach them to follow Jesus. While traditional approaches to discipleship tend to emphasize Bible study and discipleship classes, classroom instruction plays only a limited role in learning to follow Jesus. Disciple-making is not so much like teaching a person to read as it is teaching them how to apply what they read in everyday life. It is not so much like solving a math problem as it is solving the problems of human existence. It is not so much like learning the science of life as it is learning the art of living. This involves investing in people, our lives in their lives, not because we know how to follow Jesus and they don't, but because we want them to join us in the adventure of learning to follow Jesus together.

The description that follows could very well describe the process of developing a new church in a neighborhood or among a population segment in a city where none previously existed. Or it could describe the process an already existing church could use to penetrate its community in order to make disciples. Disciple-making communities are places where potential *togetherness* can become reality. People joined by their mutual commitment to one another learn together how to follow Jesus. The ultimate goal is connection with *Jesus*, but most often the initial commitment is to *one another* in the formation of community. People drawn into a community of Christ-followers learn to follow him. Those who become Christ-followers learn to invest their lives in others in the process of disciple-making. It is this movement from fringe, to outsider, to insider, to core, and then back outside again that forms the substance of this chapter.

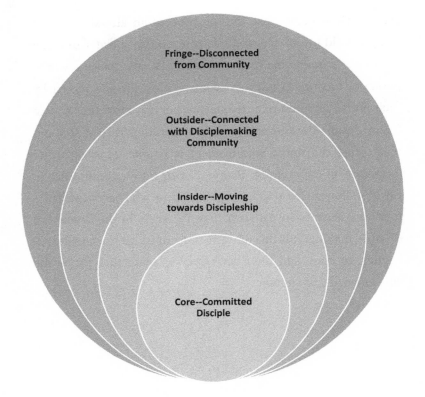

Fringe--Disconnected
from Community

Outsider--Connected
with Disciplemaking
Community

Insider--Moving
towards Discipleship

Core--Committed
Disciple

Beginning on the Fringe: Meeting Your Community

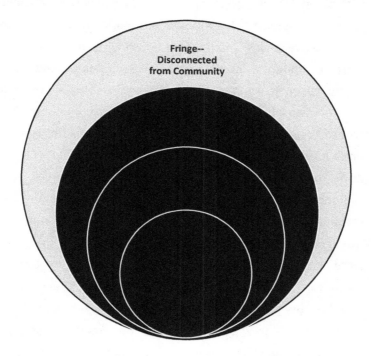

Impersonal life in today's cities can lead to a sense of "loneliness" or "isolation." While city dwellers live in close proximity to one another, they may not know their nearest neighbors. They pay little attention to another's activities as each person sets his own schedule or lives by her own rules (Scanlon, 1984, pp. 172-73). Over-concern with individual wants and needs prevents the development of commonality with others (Frazee, 2001, pp. 42-43). This may come about as a reaction against "thrown-togetherness," when people are forced to live in close proximity to others with whom they have extreme differences in culture, income, social status, and values (Amin, 2013, pp. 205-06). This discomfort causes people to isolate themselves from their neighbors. Another factor is "consumerism," which is "driven by a preoccupation to meet one's needs and to protect one's property and rights" (Frazee, 2001, p.181). This consumer culture is preoccupied with "autonomy, independence, isolation, and a longing for certainty." In their rush to be able to get what they want, city-dwellers replace the neighborhood grocer with the convenience store (Block, Brueggemann & McKnight, 2016, p. 7). In their desire to "climb the corporate ladder," social and geographic mobility cuts people off from those they have left behind (pp. 40-41). People tend to "commodify" one another, assigning values to relationships based on their ability to meet needs or satisfy wants. The result is a dehumanizing exploitation of others rather recognition of their worth as human beings created in God's image (Snyder & Runyon, 2002, pp. 144-46).

We meet people by going where they are. We must go to them because we cannot expect them to come to us. We cannot simply build a building, put up a sign, open the doors, and expect people to show up. Aside from massive media campaigns that invite people to visit celebration services at magnetic megachurches, this approach has limited value. There is little assurance of making authentic connections that will lead to discipleship. Rather than expecting people who do not follow Christ to simply show up, the church must go to them. As we meet people and listen to their stories, we come to see them as "unique and valuable" (Stetzer & Rainer, 2010, pp. 48-49). When we "do good in the lives" of people, "they come to see us as trustworthy" and the Good News we proclaim as "trustworthy" as well. This happens when we minister to their needs based on "compassion" rather than a "compulsion" to manipulate conversion (Ellison, 1997, p. 95).

This may take place through organized activities of the church in the community. For example, a church may organize a spring festival in a local park which features family-oriented food and fun. Bounce houses, pony rides and face painting are some possible attractions. The idea is to provide an afternoon of recreation for families at little or no cost. While the church may use this opportunity to publicize its location and activities, it is important to provide these activities with no strings attached. This communicates, "We care about you," not, "We are trying to manipulate you into coming to our church."

Another possibility is to carry out service projects to meet the needs of the community. This is more effective when these ongoing activities take place outside the four walls of the church. A few ideas are: an afterschool tutoring program in the local elementary school; a big-brother/big-sister program to provide mentoring for teens; a mom's day out program at a local community center; or a food delivery program for shut-in senior adults. In planning service projects, it is crucial to study the community in order to prioritize the most crucial needs. These ministries should be led by people who have the "spiritual gifts and natural talents" to carry them out effectively (Ellison, 1997, pp. 103-07).

Church members also may participate in service through community organizations rather than developing their own activities. For example, if there is already a big-brother/big-sister program, church members can simply join in rather than creating their own. If there is already an after school program in the schools, just volunteer. Participation in a park cleanup project or a neighborhood watch program are some other possibilities. Joining in already existing programs enables Christ-followers to build networks with Christ-followers from other churches, and also to develop relationships with other people who might someday choose to follow Christ.

Meeting needs takes place when Christ-followers become good neighbors with those who live around them. Sometimes this occurs spontaneously, like running an errand or watching children for someone while they run to the store. Other times more planning is involved, like organizing a cookout or a block party. In our day, when many people are reluctant to take the risk of inviting neighbors into their homes, "incidental contact" that takes place during a walk through the neighborhood or a chance meeting at the store may play a significant role in building relationships (Jacobsen, 2003, pp. 89-91). Being a good neighbor involves being willing to inconvenience ourselves in order to meet the needs of others. When we live this way, we find neediness replaced by God's abundance that is supplied through neighborly concern for one another (Block, Brueggemann & McKnight, 2016, pp. 9-20).

Connecting the Dots: Penetrating Your Community

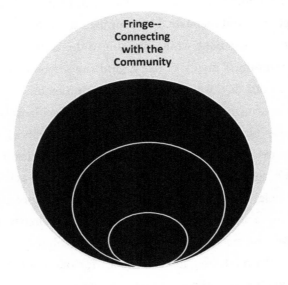

As we build relationships with people on the fringe, the church's impact among those who are disconnected will expand. The next step is to further penetrate the community outside the church by developing connections with these people. These connections take place as we form groups in the community that are exterior to the church. Initially, these groups will be formed on the basis of shared interest and geographical proximity. People who work together may meet outside of the office to enjoy recreational activities. Students who live together in a dorm may develop a wide range of social activities, ranging from sporting events to study groups. In a neighborhood, there might be a supper club for couples, a fishing group for men, an art group for youth, or a book discussion group for women. Not to be sexist, there could also be a women's auto club or a men's cooking club. When we lived in Japan, we formed a parents' night out circle with two other families. One couple would babysit the children while the other two couples were freed to have a date night. Close friendships developed between these three families that continue more than a decade later on this side of the world.

At first, we cannot expect people to share too much personal information. Participants will maintain some degree of anonymity as a means of self-protection (Harrington & Absalom, 2016, p. 87). However, these groups formed on the basis of common interest will deepen as they share life together. As people get to know each other, the distinctions between the powerful and the powerless become "flattened," resulting in "cohesion" in the midst of diversity (Sassen, 2013, pp. 213-17). As they walk with one another through life's struggles— "drug addictions, marriage problems, living as celibate singles, or overcoming habits"—they will develop "close, intimate, enduring friendships" (Harrington & Patrick, 2017, p. 74). They will develop mutual trust that leads to transparency. This will result in spiritual families that fellowship, pray, study the Bible, and serve together. Even with these activities, disciple-making will not occur unless we are intentional about challenging people to follow Jesus. Healthy groups that love and support one another speak truth into one another's lives and encourage spiritual growth through mutual accountability (Harrington & Absalom, 2016, pp. 135-43). Over time these groups will multiply, resulting in the multiplication of both disciples and churches (Cole, 2005, p. 98).

Growing from the Outside in: Forming a Disciple-Making Community

As groups multiply within geographical proximity of one another, eventually they may link with one another to form a network. A group of committed Christ-followers connected in a network realize they can accomplish more together than they can individually. When the number of Christ-followers in a community reaches "critical mass," they are able to influence the conditions of life in such broad areas as education, health care and community services. "Collective humanity cannot solve every problem or create unlimited good" (Jacobsen, 2003, p. 137). But as Christians work together to transform their cities, they can create an environment where the people who experience these benefits will be drawn to faith in Christ (pp. 130-37).

People may identify with a church for any number of reasons: they may attend with their family; the church may provide a trusted position within the broader community; there may be opportunities for social engagement; there may be support in dealing with social, family or economic issues; or, there may be a sense of shared values or cultural traditions. The nearer the church is to the cultural mainstream of the people it serves, the more likely it is that "loose affiliation" takes place. A church at the center of a culture tends to have a thin outer wall that allows people to easily pass from the fringe into the disciple-making community. So it is that in the rural South of the United States, it is relatively easy to become a member of a local Baptist church even when a person has no serious commitment to follow Christ. The same could be said for a Catholic in Argentina or an Anglican in Nigeria. In this case, church members must be continually challenged to become Christ-followers.

When a church exists on the margins of its culture affiliation becomes less attractive. A church on the margins attracts primarily those who have made a commitment to follow Christ.

As a result, a church on the margins tends to be "purer" than a church at the cultural center. However, even on the margins, everyone that identifies with a church is not a part of the core of Christ-followers. This is because family members of Christ-followers often have at least a loose connection to the church. They may participate in worship and church events and even consider themselves to be Christians, although they are not committed Christ-followers. Also, seekers may participate in worship, small groups, and other church activities in order to learn what it means to follow Christ. Based on their experience of Christian life in community with believers, these seekers will eventually decide whether or not to make a commitment to Christ. In this case, the Holy Spirit uses the lives of Christ-followers to draw these seekers to faith in Christ. This is the pattern we see in nations like Japan and India where Christ-followers face persecution from their family and society. Seekers, family members and others who maintain some connection with the church will sometimes outnumber core Christ-followers who attend these churches.

Within networks of Christ-followers, the wealthy and middle class can work with the poor to alleviate poverty and social oppression (Linthicum, 1997, pp. 176-78). These networks provide an identifiable body of Christ within the larger community where people can explore what it means to follow Christ. As this body gathers for fellowship and worship, participants find mutual support for their spiritual development. When this occurs, the form a church takes may be shaped by its calling to

> . . . demonstrate the gospel in ministry to the homeless, to young people, to the elderly, to prisoners, to the terminally ill, or to an immigrant population. Such a vocation might mean that their congregation meets in a borrowed facility, a rented hall, of a storefront that welcomes their particular constituency. (Guder, 1998b, p. 239)

Many people identify with the church, but not everyone is equally committed. There is a core of committed Christ-followers, and then other people are at various places on the continuum of following Christ. This takes place not only in roles traditionally identified with the church, such as pastor, missionary, small group leader, and worship leader, but also by people living out their commitment to Christ as "businessmen, . . . plumbers, electricians, and homemakers" (Frost & Hirsch, 2003, p 45). Christian beliefs and values become linked together when Christ-followers live in a manner that exhibits Christ wherever he places them (pp. 48-49).

Moving from Fringe to Core: Making Disciples in Community

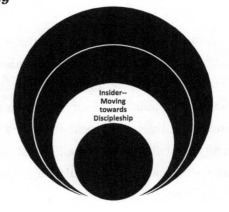

In the disciple-making process, many people in some way identify themselves as Christians. The goal is to help them move from a loose identity to become committed followers of Jesus Christ. When people come to faith in Christ, they carry baggage with them from their former way of life. This baggage varies significantly from culture to culture and results in *syncretism*—the mixture of Christianity with a person's former way of life. This may consist of the continuation of ancestral practices by converts from Buddhism, the use of incantations by converts from Voodoo, or fear of the evil eye among converts from Islam. While these forms of syncretism from other cultures are relatively easy for American Christians to spot, we are more likely to be blind to the pitfalls of our own culture where we mix Christian faith with self-reliant materialism. As people move toward the core of their Christian community, they gradually jettison this spiritual baggage.

As Christ-followers grow, they move from the fringe to the core of their faith communities. Those on the fringe are only loosely connected to Christ and to one another. Spiritual growth occurs through strengthening these relational connections. So disciple-making can never be boiled down to merely participation in spiritual activities such as worship, prayer, Bible study, and service. It is possible to participate in all of these activities and never really grow spiritually. Spiritual growth happens when Christ-followers move past Bible knowledge in pursuit of lives lived in obedience to the Bible's teachings (Harrington & Absalom, 2016, p. 173). They must put aside their differences and learn to walk with Christ together (Chute & Morgan, 2017, pp. 93-94). When "disagreements emerge," they can be used as opportunities to "build trust" and "find common ground" (Easum & Bandy, 1997, p. 154). This can only occur when group members agree to maintain confidentiality (Harrington & Absalom, 2016, p. 181). "Communities of mutual accountability" characterized by "shared insight, tangible support, and committed obedience" makes it possible to live the Christian life together in a way that is not possible for "isolated individuals" (Dietterich, 1998, p. 171). Trusting one another deeply gives way to a deepening trust in Christ, which empowers Christ-followers to carry out his mission, not only in their own neighborhoods, but also throughout their cities and around the world (Stetzer & Rainer, 2010, pp. 50-51).

The vast majority of self-proclaimed Christians are somewhere on the grid between fringe and core. They believe in the cross and resurrection of Jesus Christ as the means of their salvation and identify in some way with a local church. But they struggle with what it means to follow Christ on a daily basis.

Their lives are a mixture of vestiges of their pre-Christian ways not yet given up and traces of the new life in Christ which have taken root but not yet taken over. It is like the first sprigs of a spring garden: new life is already evident, but harvest has not yet come. The second part of this book is about this movement from planting to harvest. It is about how Christians can help one another become Christ-followers. It is about progress from the edge of Christian community to the core of Christian discipleship.

Forming the Core: Developing Leaders

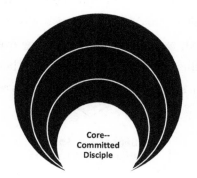

Churches often have two cores: one is a core of natural leaders who have influence in the surrounding community.

These are people with both knowledge and experience in leadership who are respected by both Christ-followers and other people in the community. But they may not have the spiritual maturity to disciple others. Those who do not follow Christ well have difficulty encouraging other people to follow him. The second core is made up of spiritual leaders. These are Christ-followers committed to the spiritual growth of both themselves and others. When a church has two cores, conflict is inevitable. The church will be pulled in two adverse directions. One measures success by worldly standards such as facilities, money and attendance. The other measures success by spiritual transformation of their community, both inside and outside of the church. The goal is for these two circles to increasingly overlap so that, as much as possible, they eventually become one. When this occurs, the church will become singularly focused on the spiritual transformation of its community.

The core of a disciple-making community should be made up of people who are firmly committed to both Christ and his church. The most important leadership quality is not charismatic personality, biblical knowledge, financial influence, or social influence in the wider community. Rather, it is the ability to reproduce Christ-like character in others. In order for this occur, those who lead must first be growing in Christ-likeness. This can be achieved when leaders inspire others to follow Christ by their example of following him (Spark, Soerens & Friesen, 2014, pp. 170-81). Bill Easum and Tom Bandy (1997) use the metaphor of "midwife" to describe this type of leadership:

> They see within others a hidden potential given by God that is greater than the potential others see within themselves. They perceive new life that is waiting to be born. . . . They are passionate to help others bring new life into the world. . . . Spiritual midwives create systems in which people can grow in faith and release creative energies for ministry. (p. 189)

Spiritual leaders must shape an environment where people are encouraged to use their gifts and abilities to carry out their passion to follow Christ. It has a "very amorphous and fluid" structure which changes constantly in response to both "internal and external forces." There is "relative freedom" for people to move in a "multitude of directions" (Brafman & Beckstrom, 2006, p. 50) under the leadership of God's Spirit. People may try "creative, innovative," even "crazy ideas" (Brafman & Beckstrom, p. 203) to bring about transformation among people in need of change.

One indication of the presence of quality leadership is how many people are carrying out "hands-on ministries" beyond their congregation (Easum, 2001, pp. 107-09). When people are released to serve using their gifts and abilities under the leadership of God's Spirit, innovative ministry "bubbles up everywhere" (Easum, 2001, p. 47). As Christ-followers serve people beyond their church, they advance disciple-making into the surrounding community. This does not mean "anything goes." Christ-followers who have been infected with the core "values, beliefs, and mission" of their church "do not need to be controlled." Rather, "trust" and "mutual accountability" releases people to "design and implement" ministries according to "their own calling by God" (Easum & Bandy, 1997, pp. 129-33).

Growing from the Inside Out: Disciples Who Make Disciples

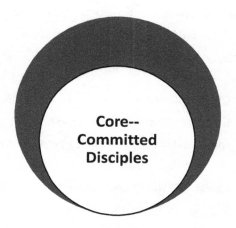

The goal is not only to develop individual disciples. Rather, the goal is to produce reproducing disciples who will produce reproducing disciple-making communities. This will take the form of networks of small groups of disciples who congregate to form disciple-making churches. These churches may take a variety of forms (see chapter 3) that fit their local communities. The measure of community fit is not merely how well local people identify with the worship and practices of the church. Fitness must be measured by the church's ability to encourage people to leave behind their old ways of life in order to move towards Christ-likeness. The two primary marks of this Christ-likeness are *loving others* sacrificially as Christ has loved us and *making disciples* who honor Christ by making disciples. This necessitates developing life-style strategies that enable followers of Christ to become the presence of Christ in their communities. A few examples are:

- Christ-followers who walk, jog, or bike through their neighborhoods, greet people they meet, and take time to get to know them through conversations.
- Christ-followers who shop in local markets and get to know the owners, employees and customers who frequent these establishments.
- Christ-followers who work in their communities rather than commuting to a job on the other side of the city. This may lead to a loss of income, but could open the door, not only to relationships, but also to many opportunities for both witness and service (Jacobsen, 2003, pp. 155-57).

A Matter of Trust

When my family and I lived in Kitakyushu, Japan, we were intentional about connecting with people in our neighborhood. I taught at a university that was a five-minute walk from our front door. Our children attended the neighborhood kindergarten. We ate in neighborhood restaurants and shopped in neighborhood stores. I had my hair cut at a neighborhood barber shop. And we mailed letters and packages at the local post office. Although we served at a church in another part of the city, we had very good relations with the pastor and people of the church that was next door to our house. We were available to assist with their ministries and served there on a number of occasions. I was not certain if all of this neighborly intentionality had any impact until one morning when I stopped by the neighborhood supermarket to pick up a few items. Earlier that morning, my wife told me she needed some money to run a few errands. I responded, "Just look in my wallet and take what you need." It was only when I looked in my wallet to pay the grocer that I realized my wife had needed all our cash! My wallet was empty, and Japan had very cash-based economy at that time. I couldn't just use my debit card to pay the bill. So without money, I apologized to the cashier and said I would need to return the items in my shopping cart. She responded (this is my rough English translation of her

Japanese): "No, that is okay, you can pay me later." I assumed she meant that I could leave my items, then come back later and pick them up when I had the money to pay for them. But when I started to leave without my merchandise, she reiterated more clearly what she intended: "Go ahead and take what you bought. Then come back and pay me later when you have the money. We know where you live. We know where you work. You are part of our community. We trust you!" Kitakyushu is a city of over a million people. I cannot imagine a large city in the United States where a cashier would tell a customer, "Go ahead and take your merchandise. You can pay later when you have the money." I cannot even imagine this taking place in the small town in Missouri where I live now. I think it was very unusual in Japan as well. What made the difference was that I was *trusted* in the community where we lived.

If we are going to become effective disciple-makers in our communities, we must be trusted by the people we live and shop and work among every day. People must understand that we will not try to deceive them or to take advantage of them. They must realize that everything we do is with their best interest in mind. Not only must we be trusted individually, but the church must also be trusted. This is not simple to achieve in places where organized religion is considered suspect and religious leaders are looked upon as charlatans. An increasing number of people in the United States believe Christianity is false, pastors are liars who are trying to develop their own reputations, and churches take advantage of the poor and vulnerable. In this hostile environment, a church must not be fueled by self-interest. Rather, the fire of Christ-like love must ignite the church to build relationships and meet needs. Only then will the neighborhood begin to trust the church. When Christ-followers are trusted, the doors of businesses and homes, and the hearts of individuals open to receive Christ's love.

Call to Action

- How would you describe the level of trust between your church and your community?
- What are some examples of *syncretism* among people both inside and outside of your church?
- If you designed a process to encourage people who do not follow Christ to move towards becoming committed Christ-followers, what would it look like?
- What would you have to do to initiate this disciple-making process in your church and community?
- What is hindering spiritual growth in your church? What needs to be done in order to overcome these hindrances?

Part Two

The Shape and Activity Of Disciple-Making Churches

Disciple-making churches vary greatly in size and shape, according to the demographics of their communities. An inner-city church will look different than a neighborhood church; and a house church will function differently than a megachurch. However, to the extent that they are effective disciple-making communities, all of these churches will have remarkable similarities of both form and function. They will almost always include some combination of large and small group experience, of celebration and cell, in which Christ-followers experience both God's glory and his love. Within this structure, discipleship takes place through the ministry of the Word, worship, fellowship, and service. As both the number and depth Christ-followers increase, they will transform their community with Christ's love.

Chapter Five
Disciple-Making Structures

It Happened One Summer

The summer of my twentieth birthday, I was sent by the Southern Baptist Home Mission Board (now North American Mission Board) to serve in a church plant in Johnston, Iowa. My experience that summer is evidence that short-term missions may have long-term impact. Until that time, I had attended traditional churches with Sunday school classes, Sunday morning and evening worship, midweek prayer meetings, and choir practice. I had never given any thought to the possibility that a "real church" might not have all of these programs. At that time in Texas, even small rural churches aspired to have Sunday school and a choir.

What I found in Johnston that summer was something completely different. This was my initial foray into the world of cell church. Merle Hay Chapel was made up of about ten members, mostly college students and young single adults who met on Sunday afternoons for worship in a rented room at a sports club. During the week, there were two cell group meetings, one for women and the other for men. What baffled me at first was they had no desire for a building, Sunday school classes, or a choir. They wanted to develop the music in their worship, but it was fine with them if they only had guitars with no piano. They hoped to multiply their number of small groups, but did not need classrooms because these groups could meet anywhere, anytime.

Through this experience, I reached the startling realization that many of the cherished traditions I connected with church might not be necessary. Maybe having one really good worship gathering on Sunday was just as good, if not better, than having two services. Maybe sitting in a circle in chairs was preferable to sitting front to back in pews. It certainly seemed to be better for getting everyone involved in what was going on. Maybe a lively, discussion-oriented Bible study was just as effective as a long sermon. At least everyone stayed awake. And I did like going to church in shorts instead of having to dress up. But what did I know? I was only twenty. Maybe what I was experiencing was only a gimmick?! Or was it real church?!

The world and the church have both changed a lot since the 1980s. What were novel ideas then have become common practice now. Drums and guitars have become more common in worship than pipe organs. Small groups of believers still meet in church classrooms, but they also meet in homes, offices, coffee shops, and college dorm rooms. Interactive Bible studies have replaced sermons in many, but definitely not all, venues.

And acceptable attire for worship varies widely from coat and tie to cut-offs and sandals.

Churches come in many different sizes and shapes as well. They vary from huge mega-churches where tens of thousands gather in stadium-like arenas to village churches gathered under trees. They may be ethnically diverse or culturally uniform. They may sing formal hymns or sway to the rhythm of drums. There is room for many different forms and patterns of church life, as long as they are communities dedicated to the task of making disciples. Disciple-making is an intentional process of calling people to become Christ-followers. This takes place through gathering a community committed to worship, fellowship, biblical study, prayer, and service, training them in

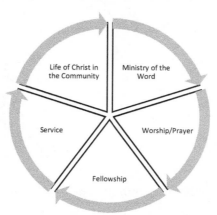

the ways of the Lord, and then sending them out to transform their neighborhoods, networks of relationships, and cities.

Some structures are needed that enable churches to carry out this disciple-making process. These structures include both large groups and small groups: small family-like groups within larger communities of believers. These believing communities are both open to newcomers, but also defined by their identity as Christ-followers. As small groups multiply, large groups expand to infiltrate growing segments of their city with Christ's love.

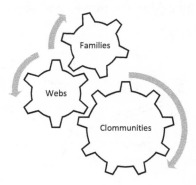

Growth of both the number and depth of disciples within a community takes place through the multiplication of small groups clustered to form congregations (Snyder, 1977, p. 123). Even when the number of churches remains essentially unchanged, the multiplication of small groups that make up these churches allows for an increasing number of venues where "more individuals [can] discover new life in Christ and new lifestyle in true Christian community" (p. 130). When these networks meet together as churches, their fellowship builds upon the intimacy that is developed in the small group setting. The result is a "highly relational and interactive" experience in which "mutual support and encouragement" extends throughout the network (Gibbs & Bolger, 2005, pp. 112-13). In this way, disciple-making which begins in small groups may eventually embrace the whole church.

Disciple-Making Families

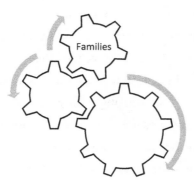

The first Christ-followers in Jerusalem gathered in small groups where they "broke bread from house to house" (Acts 2:46). During its first two centuries, wherever Christianity spread this pattern of gathering in homes continued. These early believers gathered on the first evening of the week around tables in small homes scattered throughout the cities of the Roman world for both fellowship with one another and the worship of Jesus Christ. This combination of hospitality, fellowship and worship continues to be one of the most effective means of introducing people into disciple-making communities.

During our early years as missionaries in Japan, my wife and I discovered that we could get college students and young adults to come to our house if we served food. This is by no means an earth-shattering discovery as many people engaged in ministry to young people, whether in the United States, Europe, Latin America, or Africa, have made the same discovery. Young people like to eat, and "if we feed them, they will come." Sometimes my wife and I offered our Japanese guests an American-style cookout starting with grilled hamburgers and completed with brownies and ice cream. On other occasions, it was Japanese cuisine, such as sushi or fried rice with Chinese dumplings. At other times, we simply invited everyone to bring their favorite snacks. Whatever the faire, we found that as these young people shared food together, they opened their hearts to one another as well. These times of fellowship prepared the way for in-depth Bible studies, some very transparent sharing of needs (unusual among usually reserved Japanese) followed by prayer, and consequently people coming to faith in Christ.

While forms may vary considerably with place and time, family-like small groups play a role in the disciple-making process in every setting. Some advocate only one form of small group, such as Sunday school classes, cell groups or house churches. But really there are many forms that can be used effectively in the disciple-making process. These may include ministry teams, mission teams, musical ensembles, crafts clubs, or even cadres of doctors, lawyers or educators who make their services available to those in need.

Small groups that are effective in disciple-making share a number of characteristics. They have mutual concern for one another, reflected in their desire to spend time together. The group holds one another accountable for daily study and application of the Scriptures. Not only do they pray together, they also play together. The small group my wife and I currently participate in schedules frequent meals, game nights, crafts nights, Super Bowl parties, and even fishing fellowships. Intercessory prayer for physical, financial and spiritual needs of both group participants and their family and friends is a high priority. This concern leads to service projects to meet needs both inside and outside of the group. This could be home repairs, childcare or a mission project. At times, this group life may seem hectic, but the goal is never activity for activity's sake. Rather, the small group's intention is to spur one another on to spiritual maturity.

Sunday school, dating from the late 1700s, may seem antiquated (Parr, 2010, p. 35). However, Steve Parr (2010) writes that it still works when Sunday school draws people into relationship with Jesus Christ and challenges them to follow him (p. 40). Parr (2010) describes Sunday school as "Bible study groups in local churches that are generally organized by age affinity . . . and ordinarily meet on Sunday morning immediately before or after the morning worship" (p. 14). Research among Georgia Baptists has shown that 83% of believers who participate in Sunday school assimilate into a local church. Only 16% of those who do not participate in Sunday school assimilate (Parr, 2010, pp. 18-19). When Sunday school "works," the "lost are reached, lives are changed, and leadership is developed" (Parr, 2010, pp. 23-24). Parr (2010) believes three primary factors in developing effective Sunday school are training effective leaders (pp. 98-118), reaching out to the "lost and unchurched" (pp. 121-41), and keeping "members connected" (pp. 143-70). In reaching the lost, it is important for class members to seek opportunities for fellowship with the unchurched, especially newcomers in the community (pp. 131, 136). Fellowship and caring for one another's needs are key factors in keeping members involved in the class (pp. 154-60).

Cell groups are a widely used expression of small group life. Mikel Neumann (1999) carried out a study of cell groups on five continents. He concludes that "different cultures require different approaches." A small group model exported from the United States into another culture is likely to either fail or have very limited results (p. xvii). In every cultural context, small groups emphasize: the application of Scripture in daily life, evangelism, prayer, caring for one another, and worship (Neumann, 1999, pp. 93-162). However, forms vary in different cultural contexts. For example, Neumann (1999) visited groups in Moscow that placed primary emphasis on prayer. Groups in Caracas placed more emphasis on teaching Scripture (p. 97). In a church in Chicago, priority was given "personal mentoring" to bring healing from "emotional wounds" (pp. 102, 103). New Life Church in Bombay focuses on developing new groups through evangelism among networks of neighbors (pp. 107-09). While emphases vary, small groups in every culture value relationships in which "caring concern" is expressed through "practical ministries." These ministries contribute to "effective evangelism and discipleship" (p. 146). Healthy cell groups usually have regularly scheduled meetings once a week. However, relationships between group members should extend beyond the scheduled meetings through "hangout time." This is time spent together in informal activities for recreation and fellowship (Harrington & Absalom, 2016, pp. 150-51). Harrington and Absalom (2016) enjoin, "Through these close relationships we can know each other well enough to speak into each other's lives, pray for specific needs, and enjoy God together" (p. 141).

Mission teams are another form of small group that may contribute to disciple-making. Mission teams may be either short-term or long-term; either local, domestic or international. In effective teams, "small groups of people with a common purpose" work together to develop the diverse gifts and abilities of team members (Brown, 2011, p. 145). In order to assure that needed roles are adequately filled, detailed attention must be given to the selection of team members based on both spiritual maturity and complementary ministry gifts and callings (p. 147). Mission teams are similar to other small groups in that they must place priority on developing as "communities of trust" which are bound together by: their "identity in Christ, presence of the Holy Spirit, love [for] one another, unity in diversity, [and] submitting to one another" (p. 155). Those engaged in cross-cultural mission often go through the parallel processes of cultural adjustment and spiritual development simultaneously. Cultural adjustment typically includes the four stages of "tourist, dissonance, shock, and recovery" (Decker, 2008, pp. 564-67). At the same time, the faith and identity of the person goes through the shifts of "orientation, disorientation, and reorientation" (pp. 567-75). So a person in culture shock may experience "spiritual dryness," and cultural recovery is often aided by growing sense of God's faithfulness (pp. 582-86). While cultural and spiritual disorientation results in struggle, it may also allow a person to experience God's "grace and mercy" on a deeper level (p. 586).

The point is that all small groups, even in the same church, do not have to look and function alike. A healthy church, Easum and Bandy (1997) write, will be more like "creative chaos," allowing for a multiplicity of diverse cells to meet varying needs for disciple-making within the community. Just as a healthy organism is made up of diverse cells which carry out a wide array of functions, this will be the case in a healthy church as well (pp. 107-16). While some fear that variety among small groups may lead to fragmentation in the church, this is not necessarily the case. There is room for diverse groups as long as they all share the same vision for making disciples (pp. 116-20). "Each cell is distinct," but "each cell contains within itself the imprint of the whole and perpetually seeks the well-being of every other cell" (p. 147).

Disciple-Making Webs

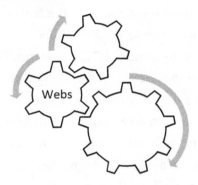

There are many churches with small groups where little real disciple-making takes place. While small groups are significant, something else is needed. What is needed is *accountability*. Every person needs someone with whom they can be completely honest without fear that information shared in confidence will be gossiped to others. Within this context, mutual encouragement comes about as people prayer together and support one another in both good and bad times. In a sense, this is what small groups are for. But the problem is that this kind of support is not experienced in every small group. There is a need for further infrastructure to insure that what *should* take place in small groups in fact *does* take place.

Neil Cole (1999) advocates organic development of disciple-making triads he calls, "Life Transformation Groups (LTGs)" (p. 53). Cole believes that as small groups increase in size, it becomes more difficult to maintain "close-knit relational bonds." The best way to maintain these bonds is to introduce smaller groups made up of three people. These triads add much needed infrastructure to groups while also allowing for a high level of accountability, confidentiality and flexibility. It is easier to find a meeting time for three people than it is for ten or twenty. And it is easier to keep information private. Also, new groups can be reproduced easily with the addition of only one or two new people (pp. 50-52). Cole believes that LTGs are most effective when they focus on only three activities: accountability through mutual confession of sin, Bible study and intercessory prayer. Accountability can take place through simply asking one another a series of questions. If participants are honest, this can result in mutual confession which will help to break "patterns of sinful behavior" (pp. 63-70).

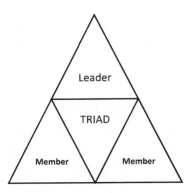

There are three advantages to Cole's disciple-making triads. *First, since the structure is simple, triads can be formed and function with very little training.* A little coaching on the use of accountability questions, intercessory prayer and inductive Bible study methods is all that is necessary to get a group, or several groups, off and running (Cole, 1999, p. 63). Of course, more advanced training may come later, but the need for training will arise out of the experience of the groups, and so will be more productive than it would be to provide complex training at the beginning. *Second, triads reproduce easily.* As triads begin to develop, they can easily spread throughout a community. Those outside of LTGs see the transformation that takes place and decide they want to be part of a group (pp. 92-94). With a little coaching, new triads begin. What begins as a small flame becomes a raging fire! As the triads reproduce, they become an expanding web of relationships that provides the basis for the multiplication of small groups and eventually churches. *Third, triads integrate evangelism with disciple-making.* It is possible for Christ-followers and those who have not made a commitment to follow Christ to participate in a triad together. Nonbelievers come to faith through "relationships of accountability" with those who are already committed to follow Christ (pp. 81-83)

A few years ago, in my disciple-making class at Southwest Baptist University, I noticed that most of the students were struggling with their own spiritual growth. Since they were not growing disciples, they were ineffective in their attempts to disciple others. In order to address this issue, I began to require my students to enter into accountability relationships with one or two other Christ-followers. Most students formed accountability triads with other students in the class, much like those described by Neil Cole. However, if students already had other accountability partners, I did not require them to participate in a new group. I did require them to enhance their level of activity to at least the level Cole mentions in his book: through mutual confession, Bible study and intercessory prayer. As a result of this new emphasis on accountability, almost all of my students began to grow spiritually. And they were energized to encourage other people to grow spiritually as well.

There are two closely-related, potential weaknesses of these disciple-making triads. One is that the three people who participate in a triad may become a clique, turn inward and become isolated from their church and community. This may lead to privatized interpretation of the Scriptures that does not line up with the historical teachings of the church. In order to prevent these difficulties, it is important to maintain a system of accountability among triads. This may be done in two ways. First, each triad should continue to participate regularly in a small group for fellowship, prayer, worship, Bible study, and service. As a matter of fact, it is a good idea if what is done in the small group and within the triad take place in complementary ways. For example, a triad can discuss the small group's Bible study in more detail. Or a triad may take on a specific role in their small group's ministry of service. Second, triad leaders can meet together with one another for accountability, to share insights and issues, and to pray together. If a small group of twelve consists of four triads, the four triad leaders can meet together once every two or three months for encouragement. And twice a year, church-wide training events could be held for triad leaders.

We also need to form "constellations" of relationships, including "upward mentoring" with those who are more spiritually mature, "downward mentoring" with those who are spiritually younger than we are, and "lateral mentoring" or "co-mentoring" with peers (Stanley & Clinton, 1992, p. 162). Upward mentors include "spiritual guides and counselors" who can guide us in important life decisions, develop strong foundations in spiritual disciplines, and help us to discover and use our spiritual gifts (p. 163). Downward mentoring of those who are spiritually less mature challenges us to continue to grow as we orient ourselves to serve others. We cannot become complacent when someone coming along after us is pushing us to grow (pp. 164-66). Finally, peers can be "more relaxed, relevant, and open with one another" (p. 166). This allows for a "confidential" level of sharing that is often not possible in other relationships (p. 166). With peers, there is a possibility for "shared experience" which allows for a higher level of "vulnerability," which brings about "mutual empowerment" (pp. 170, 175). When this level of accountability takes place, it becomes difficult to hide sin (p. 186)

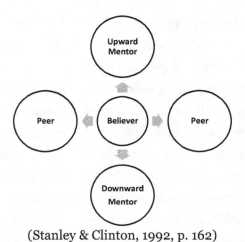

(Stanley & Clinton, 1992, p. 162)

No one who is truly committed to Christ begins the Christian life with the intention of becoming anything less than a faithful Christ-follower. But many people who begin with the best intentions grow cold. They stop growing. They stop serving. They become a life-less lump occupying space on a cold pew. And eventually they may disappear from church life altogether. The number of people who say they are Christians, but who are no longer actively involved in church and have no interest in ever going back is staggering! It is easy to say that they, like the Christians in Ephesus, have "lost their first love" (Rev. 2:4). In many cases, participating in a network of disciples where they can be held accountable, share their struggles, and pray, fellowship and serve together, can help these people grow into faithful Christ-followers.

Those who have been trained in individualized one-on-one methods of disciple-making may ask, "Why do we need disciple-making webs, triads and constellations? Isn't disciple-making just teaching people how to follow Jesus?" The answer to the second question is: "Yes, disciple-making *is* teaching people how to follow Jesus." But this explains the very reason *why* we need webs and constellations. When I attempt to disciple another person, they will hopefully learn to imitate Christ's holiness, His love, His grace, and His sacrificial service for others. But unless I am perfect (which I am not), they will also pick up at least some of my fallen-ness. In this way, they may very well become an imitator of me as well as a follower of Jesus Christ.

However, if we can develop as Christ-followers in the midst of a host of mentors, some ahead, others behind, and still others peers, we can learn from the strengths of a variety of Christ-followers. This may help us to mitigate against following the examples of weakness we observe in individuals. From a gifted evangelist, we can learn to share our faith. From a prayer warrior, we can learn to pour out our hearts in intercession for others before the throne of God. From those who are good at marriage, childrearing and finances, we can learn these skills.

From those who have a heart for the world, we can learn to live the Great Commission wherever God places us. No one person, other than Jesus, can teach us how to do all of these things well. But the whole body of Christ, using their gifts, abilities and passions for service in the context of Christian community, can help us to become more Christ-like than otherwise would be possible.

Disciple-Making Communities

There is no guarantee that the formation of small groups of people and webs of relationships will produce growing disciples. If we are not careful, we may develop a "narrow, superficial, selfish sense of well-being" while "insulating ourselves" from the "lost and hurting people all around us."

This results in what Michael Slaughter and Warren Bird refer to as "church lite." "We sing songs from the heart, we study the Bible with passion, and we tell our [inspiring] stories." But we do not make any real difference in the lives of people around us (Slaughter & Bird, 2002, pp. 215-16). To guard against this tendency towards superficiality, churches must form "relationally intentional environments" that exist for the purpose of making disciples in community "share life" together in a context that includes both "worship" and "witness"— sharing God's Word as we celebrate His grace with one another (Snyder, 1996, pp. 118-27). The gathered community worshipping God together is lifted above the concerns of everyday life to "focus our eyes on God Almighty." The mundane melts away as superficial when the glory of God becomes primary (pp. 122-23). As believers encourage one another to reflect the character of Christ, the community's witness for Christ increases as the "inevitable and necessary fruit of a worshipping, nurturing community" (p. 124).

The church as a community of Christ-followers is a very different experience than institutional expressions of church that many of us have experienced. We often speak of "going to church" as going to a place or attending a meeting. But when church is a *community,* we cannot "go to church." This is because wherever Christ-followers are scattered throughout their cities, in their neighborhoods, schools and workplaces, there is the church. Gibbs and Bolger (2005) write that the church is a "community of continuous interaction that include[s] a range of activities related to every aspect of life" (p. 100). Once or twice a week, a church may be gathered in a particular place for worship, fellowship and teaching. These meetings "support the life of the community and flow out of the community, but they do not create the community" (Gibbs & Bolger, 2005, p. 102). Seven nights a week, the church may be scattered in homes, coffee shops, restaurants, and offices, for fellowship, worship, service, and training. At other times, the church is at work in offices, schools, shops, and clinics, as Christ-followers serve others by living out their vocations. On other occasions, the church is playing in parks, ballparks, game rooms, and living rooms scattered throughout the city. Within this community of faith, people form relationships for mutual accountability—triads, small groups and webs—not to meet a requirement, but to satisfy their hunger for relationship with Christ and others who follow him (Gibbs & Bolger, 2005, p. 105).

Worship as gathered community is the most public expression of church. However, it is also the most private in that, when we gather with many others, we reveal the least about ourselves (Harrington & Absalom, 2016, pp. 64-65). While our desire to maintain privacy creates some limitations, public worship serves at least three purposes in the disciple-making process. First, our faith in God is *"inspired"* through the shared "energy, enthusiasm, and celebration of the crowd." As we experience being part of a "big family of families," we are empowered by the "presence of God" to "follow His will . . . even in difficult circumstances" (pp. 71-72). Second, the gathered community develops *"momentum"* to carry out Christ's mission of making disciples in our "street, neighborhood, and workplace" (pp. 74-75). Third, public worship provides an importance context for the *proclamation of God's Word.* This "preaching" is meant both to "encourage" listeners to have faith in Christ and to "challenge" them to live in a manner worthy of the Gospel (pp. 75-77). Harrington and Absalom write that while public worship will not be the "pinnacle" of the disciple-making process, it will encourage the "day by day, hour by hour," life on life disciple-making that takes place in other contexts (p. 89).

For people who come into our churches to experience the change that is possible through a relationship with Jesus Christ, we must develop an "inclusive and open-ended hospitality" that "welcomes and makes room for the curious, the skeptical, the critical, the needy, the exploring, and the committed" (Guder, 1998b, p. 243). Trying to develop such varied a community that attempts to be all things for all people will no doubt tax a church's limited resources. Since people are on a "pilgrimage," we must the structure of the church to continue to change with them (pp. 245-46). We must "allow the rhythms and lifestyle patterns of the people we are trying to reach determine the shape of our communal life" (Frost & Hirsch, 2003, p. 63). In other words, we must allow relationships to form naturally within the church in a way that fits the broader connections within the neighborhood or community. This may take a wide variety of forms such as:

- Living as the presence of Christ in the community
- Working together with non-Christians to solve community problems such as those related to families, young people and the poor
- "Demonstrating Jesus" through service that meets real needs
- Discussing how the Gospel responds to real life issues in settings that are neutral and non-threatening, such as over coffee or the dinner table (Frost & Hirsch, 2003, pp. 73-74)

The church scatters into its surrounding community, bearing witness to the joy it experiences when it gathers to worship Christ. It is the gathering for worship that enables the scattering for witness and service, and the scattering which enables an ever-broadening circle of Christ-followers to gather around His throne for worship. This continual pulse of life enables the church to remain faithful to its calling to make disciples (Guder, 1998b, pp. 231-32).

Call to Action

- **What experiences have challenged your understanding of church as a disciple-making community?**
- **How does your small group make disciples?**
- **Do you participate in a web of relationships that challenges you to grow spiritually?**
- **If so, how could strengthen this web of relationships?**
- **If not, what steps could you take to develop a disciple-making web?**
- **How can your church develop a healthy environment for disciple-making?**

Chapter Six
Witness of the Word

Meeting in the Upper Room

I had been invited to El Salvador to teach church leaders in the El Salvador Baptist Association about evangelism. On the appointed day, about forty people gathered in a large upper room over the association offices. The group included pastors and lay leaders, men and women, seminary professors, a medical doctor, a coffee farmer, a lawyer, an architect, and some students. As I began to share from God's Word, the Holy Spirit began to work. About two hours into our study, a number of pastors called us to a time of prayer. They said, "We cannot continue this study until we ask the Holy Spirit to forgive us for disobeying his leadership. We have tried to reach our people with the Gospel. But we have tried to do it in our own strength. We must stop trying to do God's work by ourselves. We must begin follow the leadership of God's Spirit."

This story illustrates how God's Word is central in the process of making disciples. The Holy Spirit guides us in understanding God's Word. He carries out his work through people who share with one another in community, both as congregations and as small groups. This occurs through an understanding of the Word that leads to application in daily life.

Understanding is essential, but spiritual development comes through application of God's Word. This includes both the initial decision to follow Christ and continued growth towards Christ-likeness.

The True Gospel

The Gospel is the "Good News" of salvation by God's grace through faith (Eph. 2:8). The core of this message is the death, burial and resurrection of Jesus Christ (1 Cor. 15:3-4; Hull, 2016, pp. 24-26). In the Bible, the Gospel comes to us in the form of stories. However, recent evangelism methods often reduce these narratives down to "four points and a prayer." The most recognizable form of this summary is Bill Bright's popular tract, *The Four Spiritual Laws*.

- "God loves you and has a wonderful plan for your life.
- Man is sinful and separated from God. Therefore, he cannot know and experience God's love and plan for his life.
- Jesus Christ is God's only provision for man's sin. Through him you can know and experience God's plan for your life.

- We must individually receive Jesus Christ as Savior and Lord; then we can know and experience God's love and plan for our lives" (Hull, 2016, pp. 29-31).

There have been other attempts to reduce the Gospel to make it more understandable to the average person. The most common version is to equate the Gospel with belief in religious facts about Jesus, joined together with a simple prayer, and perhaps baptism. All that is needed is a one-time experience. It is a ticket to heaven with no expectation of following Christ during this life (Hull, 2016, pp. 33-34). Another common view is that Jesus was a primarily social reformer so his followers should have the "goal of transforming society through social justice." Spiritual aspects of salvation, such as forgiveness of sin and eternal life are either downplayed or entirely overlooked (pp. 34-35). The problem here is "no one can live out the ethics of Jesus without the transcendental experience of knowing Jesus personally" (Drummond, 2002, p. 63). A third view is the "prosperity gospel," which teaches God promises "health and financial wealth" to those who "name it and claim it." Those who have enough faith can manipulate God into giving them what they want (Hull, 2016, pp. 35-36). Another view, closely related to both "belief in facts" and the "prosperity gospel" is referred to as the "consumer gospel." God is a god of convenience who exists to bless us, to give us what we want, and to make us happy (pp. 36-37). Otherwise, God is an "uninvolved Creator" who leaves us alone to "do our own thing." This type of "self-sufficiency" is really "practical atheism" (Drummond, 2002, pp. 54-55). Finally, among conservative Christians, and perhaps as an over-response to the other views, there are those who see salvation as a result of adherence to "correct doctrine" and a "narrow moral code." Being a Christian is believing that right things *about* Jesus and doing the right things *for* Jesus rather than following Jesus (Hull, 2016, pp. 37-38).

It is difficult to counter this variety of views because we live in a culture that has a predisposition against "authority" and in favor of "relativism." When truth is interpreted on the basis of personal experience, each person may claim the validity of his or her faith without invalidating the truth claims of other people (Reno, 2002, pp. 62-65). The problem with this individualistic approach to truth is it leads to a sense of disconnection from others that fails to "nurture hope in the human heart" (p. 70). What is left out of all of these views is the commitment to follow Jesus which grows out of the "courage of obedience" (p. 71). When we commit to follow Christ, he gives us new life and enables us to do his will through the work of Holy Spirit (Hull, 2016, p. 49). We are "constrained both by love of God and love of neighbor to bear witness" to this truth in both word and deed (Turner, 2002, p. 83). This brings about a "re-ordering of community" as people are "reconciled with one another" through the "power of forgiveness" (Turner, 2002, pp. 91-93).

One of the clearest depictions of the meaning of this Gospel is Peter's sermon on the Day of Pentecost (Acts 2:14-38). Peter uses as his text Joel 2:28-32 from which he draws three main points. First, God promises to pour out his Spirit on all people. Second, as a result of God's Spirit, men and women will proclaim God's Word boldly. Third, as a result of this Spirit-empowered proclamation, those who "call on the name of the Lord will be saved" (Acts 2:21). Peter's point is that the people gathered in Jerusalem have witnessed the fulfillment of Joel's prediction. At this point, Peter moves into the application portion of his sermon. Contrary to some contemporary preachers who are non-confrontational in their approach, Peter is very confrontational. His points are very direct.

- God sent his Son (Acts 2:22)
- You rejected God's Son, so you killed him (Acts 2:23)
- God raised Jesus from the dead (Acts 2:24, 32)
- Jesus, whom God raised, sent the Holy Spirit whose actions you have witnessed (Acts 2:33)

- Repent from your sins and be baptized as an act
  of faith in Christ (Acts 2:36-38

The narrative in Acts 2:36-38 clarifies the nature of the repentance that results in salvation. Repentance usually is considered to be turning away from sin in general, such as turning away from lust, broken relationships and an unhealthy lifestyle. There is certainly a place for this type of repentance as an aspect of spiritual growth. The problem is that turning from these sins *cannot* save us. A person can turn away from his or her former lifestyle and still be an unsaved sinner separated from God. In Acts 2, Peter is not talking about repentance from *sins* in general: he is talking about turning away from a *specific sin*. That is the sin of rejecting Christ. Peter is telling the crowd gathered on Pentecost that they must stop rejecting Jesus and begin to believe in him. Not only must they believe in Jesus as God's Son. They must believe in Jesus enough to follow him. This is true for us as well. We must turn from a life lived for self to a life lived for Jesus Christ (Malone, 2018).

It is not enough for people to believe what the Bible teaches about Jesus, such as Jesus' virgin birth, his sinless life, his miracles, and even his death on the cross and resurrection from the dead. As significant as these beliefs are, a person may believe all of these things and still die separated from God by sin. Unless a person trusts Jesus enough to follow him, she will not be saved. This most often occurs within a community of believers in which people experience together "authentic connection" with Jesus (Malone, 2009, pp. 49-50).

This change in direction leads to eternal results, especially "deliverance from sin" and death and "reconciliation with God" (Drummond, 2002, pp. 109-12). These are, in reality, two sides of the same coin. Jesus said those who "continue in [his] word" are his "disciples" who are "set free" by the truth (John 8:31-32). "Eternal life" comes through knowing God and his Son, Jesus Christ (John 17:3). God is the source of life. As long as we are estranged from God, we are subject to death because we are cut off from the source of life. But when our relationship with the life-giver is restored, this personal knowledge of God causes the death within us to begin to die. Eternal life takes root and grows to fruitfulness as we come to resemble more and more the character of Jesus Christ (John 15:5-8; 1 Cor. 15:19-26; Eph. 4:15). When we are reconciled with God, we become participants in God's mission of reconciling the world through the Gospel of Jesus Christ (Drummond, 2002, pp. 114-15).

The Spirit's Witness

God has given us this task to make his Word known. However, we cannot complete the task only by our determination. We "are unable to obey" without the empowering presence of the Holy Spirit. The Holy Spirit is the

"Spirit of Christ" in us (Rom. 8:9; Matt. 28:20). We can do "all things" through Christ's strength (Phil. 4:13), but without him we can do nothing (John 15:5). We must "acknowledge that we are nothing and he is all" (Fish & Conant, 1976, p. 79). Everything we do must be in response to the "guidance, leading and, discernment of the Holy Spirit" (Choung, 2012, p. 230). Otherwise, ultimately we will be ineffective in sharing the Word with others.

God's personal involvement in communication through his Word begins with his act of *inspiration*. According to 2 Peter 1:21: "No prophecy was ever made by an act of human will, but men moved by the Holy Spirit spoke from God." 2 Timothy 3:16 also confirms that "all Scripture is ispired by God." This means that God's Spirit moved human authors to write the Scriptures, so the words are God's instrument to speak to us. As a result, the Bible is the "authoritative norm" for Christian belief and practice (Grenz & Franke, 2001, p. 65).

The Spirit's witness through the Word continues in the process of *illumination*. Satan has "darkened" human hearts so that we can no longer clearly understand divine truth (Rom. 1:18-23; 2 Cor. 4:4). Yet God provides the Holy Spirit to guide us to the truth (John 14:26). This truth is God's glory revealed in Christ (2 Cor. 4:4-6). As Grenz and Franke (2001) write, "Through scripture, the Spirit continually instructs us as

Christ's community in the midst of our life together as we face the challenges of living in the contemporary world" (pp. 66-67). Their point is that the Spirit's instruction through God's Word usually occurs in the context of community as we consider his message together.

God's Spirit uses his Word to speak to both those who follow Christ and those who don't. The Spirit leads and empowers Christ-followers to bear witness for Christ. Jesus instructs his followers: "Do not worry about . . . what you are to say, for the Holy Spirit will teach you in that very hour what you ought to say" (Luke 12:11-12). "You will receive power when the Holy Spirit has come upon you, and you shall be my witnesses" (Acts 1:8). The Holy Spirit empowers Christ-followers to be effective in sharing God's Word (McRaney, 2003, pp. 28-29). As a result of the Holy Spirit, God is not limited to using only those who have theological education or ministry training. Rather, he can use "simple people" to accomplish "his purpose of blessing all mankind." The primary requirement for participation in Christ's mission is not training, but rather "prompt obedience" to his Spirit. It is this willingness to be guided by the Spirit that sets the church apart from the world (Escobar, 2003, pp. 122-23). And it is presence of "Christ's character" that enables us to determine where his Spirit is at work (Escobar, 2003, p. 124).

The Holy Spirit also works in listeners "drawing to Christ" (John 6:44), "revealing truth" (Rom. 1:18-20), and "convincing of truth" (John 16:8-11). "Without the Holy Spirit working," people would remain "spiritually blind" to the truth of God's Word (McRaney, 2003, pp. 30-31). This Word is alive, not only because it is the result of Spirit's work, but also because it reveals the truth about Christ (Malone, 2006, p. 214). I provide a good summary of the result Spirit's work through God's Word in my book, *Hearing Christ's Voice.*

> The role of the Holy Spirit is to take the things of Christ and make them known to us (John 16: 14). The Spirit takes God's truth that has been revealed through Christ and brings it to life in the human heart. . . . When the Spirit is finished, what was cold is now warm; what was not moving now has a pulse; what was dead is now very much alive and will be alive for all eternity. The Spirit does all of this by using the truth of Christ to move the human heart. This is something only God can do! (Malone, 2006, p. 206)

The Spirit's work does not end when people receive God's truth and turn to faith in Christ. The Spirit also affirms the truth of God's Word by means of *sanctification,* through which

Christ-followers are transformed into his image. "When we conform to what the Holy Spirit teaches . . . our response to the Spirit's work produces the work of Christ in us" (Malone, 2006, p. 56). Human beings cannot remain passive in this process. We must *act* in obedience to Christ in accordance with biblical teaching under the leadership of God's Spirit (Hull, 2016, pp. 103-05). The Holy Spirt does this by changing our wills so that we no longer yield to temptation, but rather act in obedience to Christ (pp. 114-22). God's Word plays a determinative role in this process. The images that fill our minds direct our actions. It is only to the extent that our minds are filled with the things of God that we learn to live in accordance with his will. So, "whatever is true, whatever is honorable, whatever is right, whatever is pure, whatever is lovely, whatever is of good repute, if there is any excellence and if anything worthy of praise, dwell on these things" (Phil 4:8).These godly thoughts come to us when his Spirit teaches us through his Word (Hull, 2016, pp. 127-28). When the Holy Spirit teaches us to obey God's Word, he draws us into Christ's work. In this way, we become streams of God's grace in a thirsty world (Malone, 2006, p. 70).

Telling God's Story

In most small groups that I have participated in, we read the Bible, then we read a book about the Bible, then we discuss what we have read. This approach uses "literate communication styles"—"the printed page, exposition, analytical and logical presentations" to enable participants to understand God's Word. The problem with this approach is that we live at a time when most people prefer *hearing* to reading as their means of communication. There are over 4 billion oral communicators in the world today (ION, 2004, p. 3). While many of these are people with limited literacy from developing countries, this number also includes "post-literates" from advanced societies. A *post-literate* person knows how to read, but chooses to not read as their preferred form of communication. For example, a 2004 survey found that 58% of high school graduates and 42% of university graduates never read another book after the completion of their education. Rather, they prefer to receive information from "non-print media" such as television and the internet (pp. 56-57). Non-literate people, whether illiterate or post-literate, process information that is "concrete, sequential, and relational." In other words, information makes sense when it fits real life experience, takes story form, and comes to them through trusted others (pp. 22-27). Often the most effective means of communicating God's Word is to tell biblical stories that "answer the essential questions of life" (2004, p. 35).

There is also a need for storytelling among people we usually consider to be biblically literate. Dan Kimball tells the story of a pastor teaching a senior adult Sunday school class to people who had gone to church their whole lives. These people knew Bible stories, but they did not understand how the whole biblical story fits together (2003, p. 188). I have discovered the same thing teaching university students that have grown up attending evangelical churches. While they recognize individual Bible stories, they lack an understanding of the grand narrative of Scripture. They have little understanding of the relationship between the Old and New Testaments, and how Jesus fulfills both the history of Israel and the words of the prophets.

Jesus always used *oral methods* to teach and most of the time he told *stories*. If Jesus ever wrote anything down, none remains. Rather, we have written accounts by others of what Jesus *said*. Paul Koehler (2010) writes,

[Jesus] created parables as fascinating stories, using plot, characterization and dialog. His spoken words were full of memorable sounds that delight the ear. He took well-known proverbs and outdid them with new proverbs of his own making, linking his new saying with the old ones so they would be easy to remember. In this way, even without writing his teachings would easily transfer from person to person. (p. 32)

There are three primary ways that biblical stories have been used in contemporary teaching.

- To provide moral examples that illustrate, either positively or negatively, consequences of particular actions. Teachers in India may use the stories of the Lost Son (Luke 15:11-32) and Noah (Gen. 9:20-29) to talk about the negative consequences of drunkenness, or the story of "Nebuchadnezzar's image" (Dan. 3) or "Elijah of Mt. Carmel" (1 Kgs. 18) to illustrate the problem of idolatry (Koehler, 2010, p. 65).

- A similar approach is to use stories to provide doctrinal teaching. For example, the stories of Jesus' crucifixion and resurrection can be used to teach his victory of sin and death, a central aspect of the doctrine of the atonement. The story of the great fish (Jon. 1) can be used to teach that God is Creator who is omnipresent and unlimited power over nature. This allows us to explain "complex theological concepts" using concrete language (Chan, 2018, p. 185).

- While these two approaches are similar and have a long history, a third more recent approach is "chronological storying." This approach was developed by missionaries working in illiterate cultures in the 20th century as a means of teaching Scripture to illiterate peoples who do not have the Bible in their language. Sometimes referred to as "Creation to Christ," this approach begins with the stories of creation in Genesis and progresses through the stories of Jesus' birth, ministry, death, burial, resurrection, and ascension in the New Testament. The intent is to provide an overarching account of the biblical witness in order to enable people to make an informed decision to follow Jesus Christ (Koehler, 2010, pp. 73-74).

After telling biblical stories, we can ask questions to find out how much people understand, such as: "What did you like about this story?" and, "What was difficult for you to understand?" Then we can probe deeper with other questions like: "What does this story teach about Jesus?" and, "What does this story encourage us to do?" These questions are meant to generate discussion and pave the way for conversations (Chan, 2018, p. 60). Listeners also "generate their own questions." This leads to "contextualized evangelism" in which we answer "questions relevant to each person's existential, emotional, and cultural contexts" (p. 184).

Telling Our Stories

We need to tell *Bible stories* that enable people to understand God's character and how he was at work in the world during biblical times. We also need to tell *personal stories* about how the same God is at work in people's lives in the world today (Frost & Hirsch, 2003, p. 101). Sam Chan (2018) provides a five-point outline to simplify preparing and telling personal stories:

- Introduce yourself
- Explain what you tried to do or how you tried to live. Include why you failed or how you fell short of your expectations, and the expectations of God and other people.
- Explain what Jesus has done for you: how did Jesus succeed where you failed.
- Explain how this caused you to decide to follow Jesus OR deepened your relationship with Jesus.
- Explain how your life is different because of the change Jesus brought (p. 56).

Some people restrict the use of personal stories to testimonies of how they came to faith in Christ. However, as Christ-followers we also should have recent stories about how God has blessed us, what he is teaching us, his protection, and other examples of his intervention in our lives. If our only story is about our how we came to salvation twenty years ago, listeners may wonder if our claim to have a relationship with Jesus Christ is true. While our conversion stories have eternal significance, my observation is that recent stories grab the attention of others, especially nonbelievers. Those who do not follow Christ often have experiences similar to those of Christ-followers, but without the difference that God's entering into the story makes. This creates space for conversations in the context of trusting relationships. Many Christ-followers are reluctant to share about what God is doing in their lives. However, sharing these personal stories may lead to opportunities to reflect upon and discuss biblical stories on a deeper level.

This type of personal story is different from most stories people tell about themselves. In most personal stories, the story-teller is the "hero." But in these stories, Jesus is the hero. The goal is to draw people to Jesus rather than to get attention for ourselves (Chan, 2018, pp. 55-57). These stories should provoke a "sense of awe and wonder" that draws people towards

God. Stories about vastness of God's creation portray a sense of his glory. But so do miraculous accounts of healing and transformation (Frost & Hirsch, 2003, pp. 101-03). We should invite people to explore how God works among us, not only through the miraculous, but also through the everyday "transformation and growth, vitality and freshness" that he brings into the community of faith (p. 105). Most of all, we need to "focus on Jesus." We need to talk about who Jesus is and what he did. We need to call people not only to *believe* in him, but also to become *Christ-followers* who live Jesus' way of life (pp. 105-07).

There are a number of advantages to teaching through stories. One is that they are more easily remembered than abstract presentations and thus more likely to be repeated by listeners to family members and friends. Nonbelievers who listen to Bible stories are temporarily drawn into the biblical world of Jesus, miracles, and the resurrection of the dead. They temporarily suspend their 21st-century worldview, and only later in reflection decide whether or not they believe (Chan, 2018, p. 177). Both Christ-followers and nonbelievers are comfortable hearing and sharing stories, so even nonbelievers who do not know the Bible can freely participate by sharing their own stories. These stories relate to real life situations, which makes application easier which leads to real change in people's lives. Stories can become a basis for conversations which lead to ongoing dialog. This can result in greater participation in small groups needed for disciple-making (Koehler, 2010, pp. 157-59).

Conversations about the Word

Conversations are most likely to occur when disciples hold one another "accountable" to mature spiritually and to make other disciples (Hull, 2016, pp. 106-07). "Group discipline" helps individuals "develop personal discipline" (p. 125). Christ-followers engaged in Christian community encourage one another to follow spiritual disciplines such as Bible study, prayer, worship, fellowship, and service. Over time, these become godly habits which enable us to "break the bondage of sin" and to develop the character of Christ (pp. 126-40).

Many people outside the church struggle with trust issues. They do not trust the Bible and they do not trust Christ-followers. This is due to the cultural shift from trust in authority figures to trust in "shared life experience" (Seel, 2018, pp. 42-45). There are a growing number of "explorers" who long for a greater understanding of truth and reality. They celebrate "new discoveries," but disdain "know-it-all" philosophers and theologians. For these seekers, "pure truth is . . . not a lived experience. Human knowledge is always mixed—a composite of truth and falsehood, belief and doubt, confidence and uncertainty" (Seel, 2018, p. 49). We may gain their trust by "encouraging people to think, to question, [and] to discover" (Kimball, 2003, p. 193). Explorers have a "3-D perspective" about the nature of reality. "They embrace humility, the possibility that some angles on the truth are incomplete or inadequate" (Seel, 2018, p. 51).

We must encourage people to give Jesus "another look" (Raley, 2009, p. 120). People come to Jesus when they see the connection between their pain and his love demonstrated on the cross (Raley, 2009, p. 129). Rather than only presenting the truth about Jesus through sermons and lectures, we can invite people to join us in a journey to discover the truth together through participatory Bible study (Kimball, pp. 285-87). When our purpose is helping other people understand truth, it is tempting to turn discussions into debates: to pile up evidence to prove we are right and others are wrong. Or we may take the opposite approach by trying to affirm something in every opinion. Rather than leaning too far towards either argumentation or affirmation, we must take a middle of the road approach "characterized by trust, openness, and risk." We must be willing to "listen, think clearly about multiple points of view," and "get hurt" (Raley, 2009, p. 123). In these conversations, Christ-followers must embrace both the "complexity" of life and our own fallenness. We must admit that we do not know everything (Seel, 2018, p. 52).

In her classic book, *Out of the Salt-Shaker and Into the World,* Rebecca Manley Pippert (1979) provides guidance for Christ-followers in our conversations with truth-seekers. First, we must be willing to share our faith without trying to force others to believe. Second, we need to be natural and conversational. Third, we should use everyday words rather than Christian or theological jargon. Fourth, we should learn to ask good questions to determine where the other person is spiritually. Finally, we need to help people to think through and clarify their beliefs. Coming face-to-face with the inadequacies of their own thinking will cause some people to seek greater understanding of the truth (pp. 125-35). Pippert (1979) suggests we move conversations from the general to the specific to the theological. For example, we might begin with questions about where a person lives and his major or occupation, then move on the questions about background and special interest, before arriving at questions about spiritual beliefs and values (p. 143). I would add two words of caution to this approach: go slowly and be authentic. Rather than attempting to rush through these questions quickly in one setting, be prepared to learn about the person over time through a series of conversations. Value the other person's time, experience, beliefs, and values. If you rush "your agenda" just so you can get to your "Jesus talk" as soon as possible, the other person will smell a rat and try to get away from you as fast and as far as possible.

Certain types of questions are helpful when communicating God's Word in small groups. Some questions do not have a right or wrong answer, but let people know their participation is important, such as: What is your favorite part of the story? Or, were there any parts of the story you did not understand? Other questions clarify the meaning of a biblical story, such as: who are the main characters? What did they do? Or, what were the results? Still other questions help with application, like: (regarding the Noah story) What helps us to persevere when other people are laughing at us? Or (regarding Abraham) What are the results when you choose to trust God? We also should ask questions that stretch people's thinking so that they recognize the "mystery and wonder" of God (Dillon, 2012, pp. 105-09).

When people tell biblical stories and personal stories to one another, they are more likely to recognize how biblical stories relate to their own lives. This "stimulates curiosity" to learn more about the Bible, and raises the desire to give "greater attention to detail." "Mutual learning" deepens relationships. A sense of family develops (Dillon, 2012, pp. 102-05). "Integration into community" enables individuals to recover the "character, virtue, and values" necessary for involvement in "public discourse" (Grenz & Franke, 2001, p. 209). The formation of this type of community does not necessitate "unanimity or uniformity," but it does lead to consensus regarding "shared values" (p. 217). "People will find a story more believable if more people in their community, their trusted friends and family, also believe the story" (Chan, 2018, p. 43). People are most likely to give their lives to Jesus when they "hang out," "get to know," and share stories with other people who follow him (pp. 44-45).

God's Truth and Community in Spiritual Change

In his classic book, *Contemporary Christian Communications,* James Engel (1975) argues that people seldom turn from sin to faith in Christ instantaneously. Rather, it is usually the result of a process in which a growing understanding of God results in a change of "beliefs and attitudes." As a person's awareness of God, the Gospel, and recognition of their implications for life develop, the person comes to a point of repentance and faith in Christ. Following this decision, the process continues as the believer is incorporated into the church and grows towards Christ-likeness (pp. 73-84). This process is illustrated in the "Engel's Scale" below (Engel, 1975, p. 83).

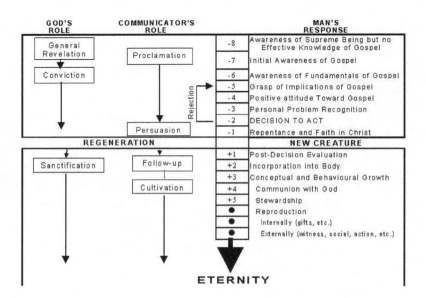

In Engel's understanding, conversion is at the center rather than the beginning of the disciple-making process. It results from weeks, months, or perhaps even years of relationship building which provides the opportunity for truth sharing. This sharing of truth is not only a human activity, but rather the result of a divine-human partnership in which the Holy Spirit "reveals and convicts" while the human witness "proclaims" God's Word. The response of the listener brings about a gradual change of "beliefs and attitudes" that begins long before a person places his or her faith in Christ and continues until the person enters eternity. The communicator's role is to take people wherever they are in this process and help them to continue to advance, not only to conversion, but to the point of becoming like Jesus (Engel, 1975, pp. 76-85).

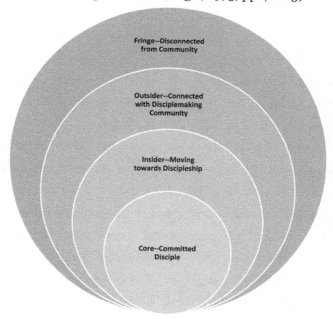

One important issue is how this individual disciple-making process connects with the process of developing disciple-making communities described in chapter 4. There is no one answer to this question. Individuals may make a personal commitment to follow Jesus Christ early in the community building process. However, there is a key transition that necessitates conversion—a definitive decision to turn aside from life apart from Christ in order to begin to follow him. That is the transition from "outsider" to "insider." This is the transition from connection with Christ's community to connection with Christ himself. Notice at this point the person is not yet a "committed disciple." The beginning steps of following Jesus are tenuous with lots of questions and perhaps even some lapses into unbelief. But it is at this point that the real laying aside of the old way of life begins.

People often are more responsive to God's Word during times of transition. Sometimes these are "times of joy," such as marriage, the birth of a child, birthdays, or times of honor for special achievements. Celebrating with people at these times allows us to build relationships that may provide opportunities for deeper sharing on other occasions. Also, we may be able to encourage people during times of stress, such as illness, the death of a loved one, or financial or relational crises. We must show genuine concern without either downplaying or magnifying the situation (Thompson, 1981, pp. 116-30). Most non-Christians are open to prayer and reading a few verses of

Scripture in their time of need. We must not overlook the potential power of God's Word to speak into the lives of individuals during these times.

Don Everts and Doug Schaupp (2008) describe a five step process that many postmodern non-believers pass through before they reach the point of trusting in Christ enough to follow him. First, they must spend enough time with a Christ-follower that they reach the point of trusting him. This leads to a curiosity about Christ and the life of those who follow Christ (pp. 29-65). Then, at some point, the non-believer becomes open to the possibility of change. This is often the most difficult step because the non-believer experiences crisis: she is confronted by both the inadequacy of her old way of life and fear of the unknown. This may result in an initial running from God until the person is driven to his knees by a sense of hopelessness (pp. 68-77). As we help non-believing friends through this crisis of belief, they begin to "seek after God." At this point, sharing stories about our faith and providing safe places to answer questions and deal with doubts is important (pp. 94-95). Small groups where people build trust by living life together can provide this atmosphere. The actual decision process of whether or not to follow Christ often lasts only about three to six months. During that time, people are open to change, and it is crucial that we do everything possible to encourage a commitment to follow Christ. Afterwards, they are either committed to Christ or "inoculated" against him (Choung, 2012, pp. 88-89). Non-believers must decide to "enter the kingdom." This decision necessitates a firm "call to commitment." People are either Christ-followers or they are not—there is no in between (Everts & Schaupp, 2008, pp. 107-12).

Call to Action

- Tell your story about how you became a Christ-follower.

- Tell a recent story about how God has worked in your life: to bless you, to protect you, to teach you a lesson, or to meet a need.

- Can you identify where two friends are in the process of learning to follow Christ (either pre- or post-conversion)?

- What biblical stories could you use to encourage these friends to take the next step in their relationship with Jesus Christ? What main points would you emphasize in these stories?

- How can your small group help one another to grow in your understanding and application of God's Word?

Chapter Seven
Making Disciples Through Worship

Why do Christ-followers worship God? It is neither merely for fellowship with one another nor for social service in the community. Either of these activities can be accomplished without worship. It is also not only to learn about God. We can study theology by simply reading a book or participating in a webinar. While our worship may be an attempt to offer praise to God, too often our brokenness prevents it (Bandy & Holmes, 2014, pp. 1-2). People have a "desire to meet God face-to-face or heart-to-heart or person-to-person" (p. 6). Yet there is no assurance that this "compulsion" will be fulfilled through participation in Sunday morning worship. People are seeking something only God can provide, but not everyone is seeking the same thing. People may be seeking: purpose in life, authenticity in relationships, a fresh start, eternal life, spiritual healing, justice, or a sense of belonging (pp. 9-10). In Christian worship, people experience God's grace to meet their needs. While these needs differ, every experience of grace is an "authentic experience of Christ" (p. 12).

Worship is "about renewing and deepening our love for Christ." This takes place when we balance "honor[ing] Christ" with "engag[ing] the heart" in a manner that is "fresh, responsive to the needs of the congregation, and not simply governed by rote performance." Worship should meet people where they are then draw them into the Lord's presence (Chapell, 2009, pp. 143-44). There are many ways to acknowledge Christ in worship:

- Communicating that we gather in response to Christ's invitation
- Verbally exalting Christ
- Acknowledging Christ's presence in word, song and prayer
- Using Trinitarian language that speaks of God as Father, Son, and Holy Spirit
- Singing hymns and songs that honor Christ and celebrate what he has accomplished through his birth, life, death, resurrection, and ongoing reign
- Using symbols, such as the cross, pictures and stained glass that remind us of Christ
- Emphasizing events in the Christian year that give special attention to Christ, such as Christmas and Easter

- Encouraging people to share testimonies of what Christ has accomplished in their lives (Cherry, 2010, pp. 32-33).

Far too often, we worship as a collection of individuals gathered in one place rather than truly worshiping the Lord *together*. We focus solely on our personal experience of the Almighty without any awareness of what he is doing in the lives of those around us. There are many ways that people can participate in worship: leadership; verbal participation in prayer, singing, reading Scripture, and reciting creeds; listening while others speak; using the senses to hear, see, smell, taste, and touch expressions of worship; and, spontaneous response to the movement of God's Spirit (Duck, 2013, pp. 20-23). However, our worship only becomes corporate to the extent we experience God's presence *together* (Chapell, 2009, p. 147).

The worship of Jesus Christ takes place "at the intersection of time and eternity." The "Eternal One" who intervened in history through the person of Jesus Christ continues to work out His eternal purpose in us (Stookey, 1996, p. 17). While Jesus' crucifixion and resurrection occurred only once as singular events in history, the transformation these events make possible continues to be actualized within Christ-followers. Worship becomes both our offering of praise to God and his gift of grace to us (pp. 29-33). As we experience the "transforming power of the resurrection," we participate in the promised "new creation" (2 Cor. 5:17; Rev. 21-22) in the here and now. In this way, the "corporate praise of the saints" becomes a "foretaste of heaven," an anticipation of the joy of eternity (Stookey, 1996, pp. 40-42).

Worship That Meets Needs

Bandy and Holmes (2014) believe different types of worship meet the needs of different people (pp. 30-32). They distinguish between seven types of worship. Each type contributes to the disciple-making process.

- *Coaching worship* provides direction for those who are lost, confused, anxious, or overwhelmed. These services provide practical advice for everyday living, such as family life, finances, and ethical decision-making (pp. 35-51).

- *Educational worship* teaches doctrine, ethical positions and church policies. This instruction is "theoretical rather than practical." Every aspect of worship—sermon, prayers, and even music—contributes in some way to the lesson that is being taught (pp. 65-71).

- *Transformational worship* brings people into a "direct and immediate experience of the Holy in such a powerful way that it dramatically changes or redirects an individual's life" (p. 85). Music, prayer and testimonies are emotionally intense and may lead to dramatic displays of God's power such as healings and other miracles. The goal is "renewal of the inner spirit, the transformation of the attitude, and the re-creation of life" (pp. 92-93).

- *Inspirational worship* gives people "confidence and courage for the future." It motivates "optimism and joy" in people who struggle with "despondence and depression" (p. 109). This occurs through a "celebration" of God's blessings. Inspiration may blend worship with "entertainment, spectacle and sport" through a combination of interesting speakers, entertaining music and expert media. When this happens, people may show up for an enjoyable experience rather than to meet with God (pp. 123-27).

- *Caregiving worship* allows people to experience "God's embrace" as "companion, protector and benefactor." Worship becomes an "oasis of rest" where God protects his people from a "hostile world." (p. 145). The church provides "mutual support" during key events such as "births, weddings, graduations, and funerals" (pp. 152-53). This occurs most often in small multi-generational churches where grandparents, parents and children fellowship, pray, worship, and serve together. Dinners shared together following worship become family meals (pp. 155-58).

- ***Healing worship*** helps people "experience physical, emotional, mental, or relational wholeness" (pp. 177). This is helpful for people who feel trapped by "poverty, crime, injustice," poor health, and other circumstances beyond their control (p. 181). Healing worship includes both the "horizontal dimension" of human support for one another and the "vertical dimension" of "God's awesome grace" intervening to relieve the sufferer (pp. 183-84). This often occurs in small, informal gatherings in which believers are more likely to show care and concern for one another and no formal structure is required (pp. 185-90).

- ***Missional worship*** motivates Christ-followers to become helpers through ministries of "community development and social activism" (p. 199). This "worship is all about mission": providing "information about mission needs, prayer for mission, and send[ing]" people on mission. The music, praying and preaching all point to the urgency of carrying out God's mission, both in the city and throughout the world (p. 205).

While worship can contribute in many ways to the disciple-making process, no single gathering for worship can be all things for all people. It is impossible to have a single gathering that will be, at the same time, coaching, educational, transformational, inspiring, caregiving, healing, and missional. On the other hand, through sharing life together we discover who God is and his love for us. Without the context of "our daily struggle to make sense of longings, hopes, fears, [and] joys," our acts of worship become "empty" (Saliers, 1994, p. 27). One option is for a disciple-making church to develop small groups that meet different needs. Some groups may focus on education while others focus of coaching, transformation, healing, inspiration, caregiving, and mission. These various ways of worship breathe God's life-giving grace into participants and enable Christ-followers to engage in mission in both their local community and the wider world.

Another possibility is to develop "blended worship." This term is commonly used to mean the blending of worship styles such as traditional and contemporary by singing both hymns and praise songs. But Bandy and Holmes (2014) use "blended worship" to refer to the blending of two purposes, such as coaching and inspiration, or transformation and caregiving (pp. 219-44). This type of blending can respond to the "complexity of human needs on a deeper level" (p. 228). This enables people to experience the power of God's limitless grace in response to the "finitude" of the human condition. When this happens, worship leads to hope for both this life and eternal life (pp. 230-31). Some worship blends go together rather naturally, such as educational and coaching worship or transformational and inspirational worship, while other blends are more difficult, such as blending transformational and educational worship or caregiving and inspirational worship. Bandy and Holmes (2014) believe that it is impossible to blend more than two types together (pp. 232-43).

Another option is the possibility of providing a balanced diet of worship experiences. A single church might provide various types and blends of worship at different times in order to meet various needs within their congregation. At various times, worship in a single church may be educational, transformational, inspirational, or missional. But we must avoid the temptation of building a worship experience around only one theme, such as "forgiveness, justice, or confession." This is because "people need the whole Gospel every Sunday" (Lowery, 1992, p. 33). Worship that meets needs "overcomes boundaries" that prevent people from meeting God in their local culture (Gibbs & Bolger, 2005, p. 75). It allows people to become "vulnerable," bringing all their "strengths and weaknesses, personality and experiences" into God's presence (Gibbs & Bolger, 2005, p. 76).

We also can move beyond the limitations of traditional worship by engaging all of the senses: for example, sight through colorful pictures and drama; smell through the fragrance of candles and flowers; hearing through songs, prayer, and preaching; taste through Communion and a fellowship meal; and touch as believers clasp hands or embrace one another in Christ-like love (Gibbs & Bolger, 2005, p. 78). Worshipers set aside their personal "satisfaction" in order to "reach out and minister to each other" (Block, 2014, p. 243). This also allows Christ-followers to invite non-believing friends into a welcoming environment (Gibbs & Bolger, 2005, p. 79).

Worship: A Journey towards Discipleship

In Luke 24:13-35, two disciples meet Jesus on the Emmaus Road. At first glance, this story is only intended to provide evidence for Jesus' resurrection. But as we dig a deeper, we notice a portrait of the regenerative quality of worship: as we walk with Jesus he changes us. In this story, Jesus "engages the disciples": he initiates the conversation and they respond to him. Their dialog is framed around God's Word and gives Jesus the opportunity to reveal his true nature. They invite Jesus to join them in fellowship. Jesus reveals himself further in the "breaking of bread," the Lord's Supper. In the end, the disciples' recognition of Jesus compels them to "tell others" about him (Cherry, 2010, pp. 15-16).

True worship is never merely a human activity. There is always a "God-human exchange" which God initiates and his people respond. It is not adequate for a congregation to sit passively, listening to God's Word preached, or to attempt to "entertain God" through their performance. People may begin as "tourists" who show up to be entertained by a performance and learn more about Christianity. But over time they can be changed into "pilgrims" called to join with others in the journey towards Christ (Duke, 2013, p. 263). They enter into a conversation in which they both hear from and respond to God (Cherry, 2010, p. 9). They move, whether this results in kneeling in humility or raising their hands in praise, following the Spirit's leadership (Webber, 1998, p. 46). In Christian worship God initiates this interaction. He speaks, then we respond. Then God sends us to continue his mission (Cherry, 2010, p. 45).

The worship model briefly described below may be utilized in a wide variety of settings: from a few friends gathered in a living room to a congregation of thousands in a huge arena. As a result, the form and feel of worship may vary, but the essential content does not. Whether we kneel in intercession around a coffee table with close friends or raise our hands in praise with a multitude of Christ-followers we hardly know, we are knit together in worship through our mutual relationship with Jesus Christ. Within these widely varied contexts, worship plays a crucial role in disciple-making.

God initiates worship. Worship is not only an instructional meeting in which we learn about God. It is actually a meeting *with* God in which he joins his people together through the inner working of his Spirit (Cherry, 2010, pp. 54-55). In this initial stage of worship, God's Spirit moves "preoccupied, self-centered, isolated individuals" to recognize who God is and what he has done. This may take place through the reading of Scriptures that remind us of the character and activity of God, singing songs of praise and adoration, prayers that confess our adoration and praise of God, and testimonies about God's faithfulness and work in the lives of his people (Cherry, 2010, pp. 55-56). This initial stage of worship may be as brief as a word of prayer calling upon those have gathered to worship God, or as long as a litany of songs, prayers, Scripture readings, and testimonies that remind us of what God has done and call upon his people to worship him (Cherry, 2010, pp. 59-62). When we hear about "God's saving deeds in the past," we are moved to consider how he may be at work among his people in the present (Webber, 1998, p. 42).

In multicultural settings, using a variety of cultural elements may communicate to people of different languages and cultures that they are welcome in God's presence. This might include Chinese calligraphy, artwork from many nations, as well as singing, praying and reading Scripture in many languages (Duck, 2013, pp. 52-53). When I attended Tokyo Baptist Church, a multi-national congregation in inner-city Tokyo, preaching took place in both English and Japanese, and worship was led by choirs that sang in English, Tagalog, as well as African languages (Tokyo Baptist Church, 2018). These multicultural expressions bring about a profound sense that the God we worship is Lord of the nations.

In contemporary worship, this initial stage is often carried out almost exclusively through music with little use of prayer,

Scripture and testimony. While music may be effective, it can be strengthened through the use of well-placed prayers, Scriptures and words of encouragement. For example, a greeting that reminds people that they have gathered to worship Him may set the tone for all that follows. Also, a time of greeting one another may help to establish the sense of community needed for corporate worship (Webber, 1998, p. 80).

Worship may begin with "gathering songs," inviting participants to fellowship with one another. This will be followed by quieter, more reflective songs, encouraging participants to enter into God's presence (Webber, 1998, p. 64). The combination of "tempo, pitch, volume, melody, harmony, and rhythm" allows us to express a greater range of emotion through singing than is possible through simply speaking (White, 2000, p. 112). "Congregational singing" allows everyone the opportunity to participate in offering praise to God (p. 113). So songs used for this purpose should be "singable," with words, tunes and rhythms easily grasped by worshipers (Block, 2014, p. 242).

Leading worship is "pastoral" in that its primary purpose is leading people into the presence of God so that they can commune with him (Block, 2014, p. 245). While form and style are important, the selection of worship music must not overlook its biblical and theological bases. It is especially important to focus our singing on the "centrality of Christ" and the "glory of God" (Block, 2014, pp. 236-37). This does not mean that all of our music must be "upbeat and joyful." This leaves the false impression that Christ-followers are always happy—something that we know is not true, and may mislead non-believers who come to worship with us. Rather, taking the Psalms as our cue, we can express the full range of human emotions in our songs of worship: not only joy, but also sadness; not only thanks, but also grief. We can "unload our burdens" on the Lord and call out for his help in our time of need (Block, 2014, p. 240).

God speaks. The proclamation of God's Word may take many forms: preaching, Scripture reading, responsive reading, or inductive Bible study are only a few examples. While sharing God's Word necessarily involves human actors, the primary actor is God's Spirit who speaks God's Word through proclaimers to listeners (White, 2000, p. 167). The purpose is not primarily to "learn about God," but rather to "hear from God" (Cherry, 2010, pp. 68-71). God is "speaking and we are listening" (p. 70). Otherwise, what takes place is no more than a lecture (White, 2000, p. 167). It also is possible to use drama, Scripture songs and art to reinforce the biblical message (Webber, 1998, pp. 91-92).

The value of Scripture in worship is not limited to using it as a basis for preaching and teaching. Since God's primary revelation comes us through his Word, our interpretation and explanation are less important than the Bible itself. So we must "devote more time to reading the Bible" rather than using it only as a "call to worship" or "preface to the sermon." Daniel Block (2014) suggests we should:

- Prepare spiritually for the reading of Scripture through prayer
- Create an attitude of reverence by encouraging people to stand for its reading
- Read large blocks of Scripture in order to help people understand the Bible's coherence
- Structure worship so that reading Scripture is given equal or greater value than its interpretation in the sermon (pp. 190-91)

In a small group, an inductive study that encourages active participation from everyone in the group may be more effective than a message delivered by a preacher or Bible teacher. We should do everything possible to insure that those who share the Word are prepared to speak. "Where gaps exist between the world of the biblical author and the modern reader, sound exposition is essential" (Block, 2014, p. 192). Training in preaching, teaching, Scripture reading, and story-telling is needed, not only for professional ministers, but for lay leaders as well (Webber, 1998, pp. 94-98). This may be done by providing either classes or mentoring for believers gifted in this area. We need to "cultivate a culture of dialog" that encourages participants "to think, to question, and to discover" based on trust between speakers and listeners (Kimball, 2003, pp. 192-93). The goal is to move the congregation from passive listening to active response to God's Word. This response may take a variety of forms: a lengthened time for prayer response; singing songs that reinforce the message; or allowing participants to ask questions and respond verbally during the sermon are a few ideas (Webber, 1998, pp. 98-104).

God calls for a response. There is no one way for a church to respond to the Lord's message. A church's response will fit what God has said to the congregation as well as the church's culture, age of participants, history, and denominational tradition (Cherry, 2010, pp. 104-05). Prayer may take many forms: "praise, thanksgiving, confession, intercession, and oblation." All of these allow us the opportunity to "express to God what concerns us most deeply" (White, 2000, p. 167). The most basic response to God's Word is "repentance" (Acts 2:38), which is "surrender to the will of God" (Cherry, 2010, p. 100). "Gratitude" includes both praise for who God is and thanks for what He has done for us. It opens us up to "God's grace . . . bestowed on us" on a daily basis (Saliers, 1994, pp. 32-33).

While evangelical Christianity has emphasized the response of the individual to God's call during the invitation, there is a need for the gathered community of believers to respond as well. This may take many forms, of few of which are: extended congregational singing of hymns and/or praise songs; words of testimony; individual, small group or congregational prayers; artistic expressions such as painting, poetry or sculpture; recitation of creeds; public readings of Scripture; and public confessions of faith in Christ (Cherry, 2010, pp. 103-04). Learning to "speak the truth in love" enables us to address our "dark side," including our "fears, fantasies, ambivalences, and doubts" (Saliers, 1994, pp. 33-34). "Solidarity" results as we lift one another up to the Lord (pp. 35-36). Through "intercession," we "counter the brokenness of the world" with the "compassion of Christ" in community (p. 132). We "suffer with our brothers and sisters" as we as express our "vulnerability" both to Christ and to one another (p. 133).

God sends the gathered church into the community. He blesses us so that he can bless others through us (Cherry, 2010, p. 112). This may be as simple as words of benediction given at the end of corporate worship: "Go and make disciples," "Go in peace to love and serve the Lord," or "Go in the grace of our Lord

Jesus Christ and the power of the Spirit to change the world for God's glory" (p. 115). This sending is "not an ending" (p. 117). Rather, it is a signal that the church scattered continues to worship God throughout the week through both our words of witness and works of service in the community. Not only religious acts such prayer, devotion and Bible reading, but also "how we live"—following "ethical norms" as well as "acts of social justice"—are acts of worship based on our faith in Jesus Christ (Saliers, 1994, pp. 172-73). Harold Best (2003) writes,

> Our worship is acceptable and effective by our being moment-by-moment living sacrifices, doing everything in the Spirit and according to the truth, seeking out the beauty of holiness as our only walk, holding fast to God, who alone is our praise and worship. (p. 41)

There must be an intimate connection between gathered worship with the church and daily worship when we are scattered throughout the community. Sacrificial giving done in response to God's Word under the leadership of his Spirit must take place in both liturgy and life.

Recovering the Use of Stories

One way we can strengthen the communication and application of God's message in worship is by recovering the use of stories. When I was a small child, I attended Sunday school classes where adults told Bible stories to children. As I grew older, I noticed people stopped telling me stories and began to try to explain the Bible. Underlying this change is the philosophy: "Stories are for children. Adults need to understand their faith." The problem is that adults as well as children are more likely to *understand* stories rather than abstract reasoning. We are more likely to *remember* stories as well. Many times I have departed worship with little memory of the main points of the preacher's sermon. But if he told a good story, I might still remember it the next time we gathered for worship.

When I taught Bible at a college in Japan, I discovered that most of my students from Buddhist families knew little about the Bible, so I told Bible stories. When I returned to the United States to teach at a Christian college in the Midwest, I was surprised to find that many students from Christian families knew little more about the Bible than their Japanese peers. So I teach them through Bible stories as well. They have attended too many Bible studies where the Bible is not taught and too many worship services where Bibles are not opened or read. From this experience, they have gained the impression that the Bible, even for Christians, is not very important. This is reinforced in American culture when people ask, "What makes [the Bible] different from all the other religious books out there?" (Kimball, 2003, p. 172).

While we want to avoid the temptation of watering down the meaning of God's Word, we must keep people's attention. This can be difficult when people are used to being entertained by five-minute information bites on television and social media. Only the very best orators can hold people's attention for more than a few minutes. Most of us must learn to make the best use of the brief attention spans we are allotted. One possibility is to break biblical teaching into five minute segments with brief "commercials" in between: personal stories and illustrations that will recapture the listeners' attention (Morgenthaler, 1995, pp. 194-95). Think of a thirty minute message as a string of five minute vignettes tied together by a series of transitions. When we do this, we should avoid "randomness" by tying each part of the message around a central theme (p. 197). For example, we could tie five vignettes together in this way to tell longer biblical stories such as Joseph's sojourn in Egypt, David and Goliath, or the crucifixion of Jesus. Or we could tell a series of stories tied together around a theme such God's Grace, loving one another, or sacrificial living.

Sharing stories allows both Christ-followers and nonbelievers to actively participate in worship. Simple statements made by nonbelievers such, "I can't believe," "I don't understand," and "I hurt," provide opportunities to share simple (or sometimes complex) stories that pave the way for deeper conversations. While Christ-followers may struggle at times to share about their weaknesses, sometimes unbelievers will openly testify about what their lives without Christ are like. The Holy Spirit "knits together" Gospel conversations between "saints and sinners" (Best, 2003, p. 80) which provide opportunities for biblical witness, prayerful intercession and confession as nonbelievers turn to faith in Christ (pp. 78-79).

Witness and worship meet together in God's Word. We must learn to tell biblical stories so they intersect with personal stories. The God who is revealed in Jesus Christ meets the hunger of the human heart (Kimball, 2003, p. 178). The Gospel includes not only God's love for the sinner, but also his hatred of sin (Best, 2003, p. 87). Rather than watering down our teaching, we can use stories to teach important biblical themes like: the disciple's life-style, salvation through God's grace through faith in Christ, the importance of marriage and family, and the trustworthiness of Scripture (Kimball, 2003, pp. 181-82). This type of teaching can be enhanced through the use of "visual imagery" such as "photos, art, graphics, and film" which draws attention from the preacher to the story (pp. 189-91).

Conversations around the Lord's Table

The most important aspect of worship for disciple-making is neither the songs we sing nor the sermons we preach. Rather, it is our Communion around the Lord's Supper which "makes visible" our love for both the Lord and one another (White, 2000, pp. 198-99). Communion is not partaking in a mystically present Christ (as in traditional Catholic doctrine), but rather a "personal encounter with the living Christ" (Bloesch, 2002, p. 163). In the Emmaus Road experience (Luke 24), the "breaking of bread" reveals the resurrected Jesus to his disciples (Webber, 1998, p. 129). In the early church, the Lord's Supper joined together Christ-followers in "covenantal relationship" both with one another and with their Lord (Cherry, 2010, pp. 11-12). The act of "breaking bread" together was the central act of worship among the earliest Christ-followers in Jerusalem and spread with the movement. Over time, it came to be referred to as the *Agape,* or "love feast," and consisted of two parts, a communal meal and the Lord's Supper (McGowan, 2014, p. 34). McGowan (2014) notes,

The meal celebrated how Jesus had brought them into community to be children of God as

Jesus was himself. Drinking and eating was
realization and reiteration of their belief that
they were God's own people, scattered now but
ultimately members of a holy, united, and
redeemed community. (p. 38)

In the Supper, we join together present, past and future: we "proclaim" in the present "the Lord's death" in the past "until he comes" in the future (1 Cor. 11:26). There are three movements which must be held in balance within a proper observance of the Lord's Supper. First, since it is a remembrance of Christ's death and resurrection, it is a time for *reflection and confession of sin.* Second, since Christ's cross-work is "finished" (John 19:30), we observe the Supper as a "thanksgiving feast," a *celebration of Christ's defeat of sin and death.* This is the significance of the Greek term, "Eucharist," which means, "thanksgiving." Lord's Supper is a time of joyous celebration. Finally, the Lord's Supper provides the opportunity for "Communion," a *celebration of the community's "oneness in Jesus Christ."* We are bound together in fellowship by Christ's Spirit because of our common experience of his saving grace (Cherry, 2010, pp. 87-88).

It is customary for churches to choose only one of these three movements for their Communion observe. Thus they are either reflective, celebratory or relational. Yet is far more effective in the disciple-making process when the three movements of the Supper are brought together into a single symphony. We begin with a time of reflection and confession, preparing our hearts for renewed communion with Christ and His church. While there is a place for confession of individual sins, what is most important is our confession that we have not been faithful in following Christ as we should: we have been disobedient; we have failed to serve others in Christ's name; we have not shared verbal witness as we should. In failing to follow Christ individually, we have also failed his church: we have not encouraged others to grow as His disciples as we should.

Second, we celebrate Christ's defeat of sin and death. At this point, we partake of the elements of the Supper with others. We remember and give thanks for the body broken and the blood shed for us. This may include much more than a simple recitation of 1 Corinthians 11:23-26. It may also include worship in prayer and song. It may even involve testimonies by individuals of how the Lord has blessed them through remembrance of his death and resurrection.

The final movement is our mutual communion with one another in Christ. While it is seldom done, I would encourage some sort of return to a fellowship meal similar to the practice of the early church. This is not only an ancient tradition. The love feast was practiced by Mennonites, Moravians and Methodists in small group gatherings as late as the eighteenth century (White, 2000, p. 235). This practice which joins together worship of the Lord and fellowship among His followers might yet again be revived. In small churches, this could take the form of a traditional potluck dinner, followed by observance of Communion around tables in the church's fellowship hall. In larger congregations, it might take the form of small groups gathering throughout the community for table fellowship in homes and restaurants.

North Americans suffer loss of the Supper's significance because we live in a culture where bread is regarded as a side dish. In first century Palestine, bread was the center of the meal and the basic necessity of life. Without "daily bread" (Matt. 6:11), people died. As the American diet marginalizes bread, Communion makes less sense. People from Asia may find that "using local elements, such as food and drink made from rice," help them to more fully connect Communion with their everyday lives" (Duck, 2013, p. 35). I have argued in my university missions courses that in cultures where rice is the primary source of daily sustenance, the use of rice rather than bread in the Supper more fully communicates the message that

Jesus alone is the source of eternal life. Communion should remind us that this life in Christ is meant to be lived together in community. Ruth Duck (2013) writes,

> Each local church must engage in its own creative process to discover how to praise more deeply, to tell the story more truly, and to enter into communion more fully. We never arrive at a perfect form of worship that remains the same forever, so it is the task of each generation, each culture, each context, to seek new ways to touch the hearts of all with the word of the gospel. (p. 270)

This level of table sharing both leads to and flows out of "mutual indwelling," more commonly referred to as *fellowship*, which is the emphasis of chapter eight. Mutual indwelling takes place when we both continually "pour out" ourselves and are "poured into" by others with whom we share life. It includes eating meals together, celebrating together, and weeping together. It draws us together to strengthen one another's weaknesses then sends us out to share good news (Best, 2003, p. 54).

Call to Action

- Which aspects of worship give you the greatest sense of the Lord's presence?
- Which types of worship are most likely to meet the needs of people in your community?
- How would you describe your conversations with God through worship?
- How can stories help you worship?
- How can Communion help you worship with others?

Chapter Eight
Fellowship: Life Together

Fellowship of the Holy Spirit

Koinonia, the Greek word usually translated "fellowship" in the New Testament, might be better rendered as "community." Koinonia is derived from the Greek term koinos, which carries the connotation of "interdependence, shared responsibility, mutual instruction, and commonality" (Dietterich, 1998, p. 146). Christ-followers are to live with "one another" (Rom. 12:5) in community marked by encouragement (1 Thess. 5:11), "love" (Rom. 12:10), instruction (Rom. 15:14), service (Gal. 5:13), and "harmony" (Rom. 12:16; Dietterich, 1998, p. 148). This "community of love" cannot remain self-contained. It "overflows" to "embrace" the neighborhood, the city and the world (p. 149).

We tend to equate fellowship with human activity. This is true whether we are referring to eating together, praying for one another, or service to meet one another's needs. All of these are things people do, either together or for the benefit of others. The reduction of fellowship to human activity forces us to carry the load of support and encouragement for one another. This is a burden none of us is prepared to bear. It is through our mutual connection with Christ that we are joined together. And it is through Christ's love at work in us that we are able to love one another as we should (1 John 4:9-11). This kind of fellowship is not the product of human effort, but is rather the result of God's Spirit at work among us.

In the final verse of 2 Corinthians Paul writes,

> The grace of the Lord Jesus Christ,
> The love of God,
> And the fellowship of the Holy Spirit
> Be with you all (13:14).

Through these words, Paul prays that divine blessing will come upon his readers. This blessing takes three forms, each from one person of the Trinity: grace from Jesus Christ, love from God the Father, and fellowship from the Holy Spirit. This passage teaches us that fellowship, like grace and love, is God's gift to us. Just as grace comes to us through the work of the Son and love through the work of the Father, fellowship is the result of the Spirit's work among us. This work of the Holy Spirit brings "healing and forgiveness" to relationships otherwise marred by sin (Dietterich, 1998, p. 146). This healing takes place as the Spirit empowers the community of believers to "manifest the love" of Christ for one another, characterized by "peace, patience, kindness, goodness, gentleness, and self-control" (Gal. 5:22; Dietterich, 1998, p. 147).

Table Fellowship

Christian fellowship has long been synonymous with food. When I was a child, a few times each year my family stayed at church after Sunday morning worship for covered-dish meals. In East Texas, these occasions brought forth an interesting blend of Southern and Southwestern cuisines: southern fried chicken with chicken fried steak, barbequed brisket with enchiladas, potato salad with taco salad. The desert table was loaded with banana pudding, peach and apple cobblers, chocolate and carrot cakes. And of course, there was always gallons of fresh sweet tea to wash everything down. While food filled our tables, plates and stomachs, the primary goal of these gatherings was to develop relationships for mutual support and encouragement. This bore fruit as church members prayed for one another, visited each other in the hospital, prepared food for the bereaved, and provided financial support for families in crisis. I still experience the results of these times together during weekly calls to my mother, now in her eighties. She inevitably passes on word of people in the church that I knew forty years ago who are either sick or have passed on, as well as word about their children and grandchildren I have never met.

This is my mom's effort to keep me in this loop of relationships and provides the opportunity for me to pray for those in need.

This relationship of food with fellowship is not limited to Christ-followers in the southern United States. The small churches typical of Japan have a strong sense of family. Their cohesion is aided by the practice of eating lunch together every Sunday. In the churches I worked with in Japan, a typical Sunday began about 9:30 a.m. with worship. This was followed by small group Bible studies and then lunch together as a church family. After lunch there would be other meetings and activities, often ending with a tea or coffee time accompanied by cakes and other snacks about 3 p.m. Many of these Japanese believers were cut off by their biological families when they chose to follow Christ. So it was very important that they provide family support for one another. The most crucial aspect of this support seemed to be quality time with one another which often occurred around the table.

Fellowship meals among small groups of Christ-followers is not a recent innovation. As we have seen in the previous chapter on worship, this practice goes back to the very first church in Jerusalem. Those earliest believers broke "bread from house to house, they were taking their meals together with gladness and sincerity of heart" (Acts 2:46). "Breaking bread" does not refer to only eating meals together. Rather, it refers to taking Communion together in the context of a fellowship meal. This meal connected horizontal fellowship among believers to the mutual fellowship that each believer shared with the Lord Jesus. In this way, they came to understand that it was through their individual relationships with Jesus Christ that they shared life together as the body of Christ.

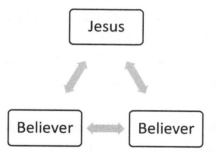

In the vast majority of churches, the Lord's Supper is a means of worship with little or no thought given to fellowship. The bread and wine (or juice) connect worshippers with the central historical reality of Christian faith—the sacrificial death and resurrection of Jesus Christ. Through the Supper, we recognize God's work of grace through his Son and we respond in faith to what he has done for us. While this remembrance of the Lord's death (1 Cor. 11:26) has eternal significance, we often fail to recognize that our mutual connection with the Lord Jesus links us to one another as well.

I believe one reason for this disconnection is our contemporary practice that separates Communion from a fellowship meal. While there are some "emerging churches" that have attempted to resurrect the biblical practice of Communion in the context of fellowship (Gibbs & Bolger, 2005, pp. 119-20), this remains relatively rare. I have participated in a wide variety of churches—house churches, cell churches, small rural churches, small city churches, neighborhood churches, and mega-churches. I have led and received the Lord's Supper in almost all of these settings. In over half a century, very rarely have I participated in Communion in a context that also included a fellowship meal. The Bible nowhere insists that we *must* break bread in the context of a fellowship meal. But I cannot help but think that because we do not, we fail to fully comprehend the nature of our fellowship, both with Christ and with one another.

During my sojourn in Missouri, I have had many opportunities to serve in rural churches. Many of these churches average thirty to fifty in attendance. While these churches are small, they are not necessarily weak. Some of them have a strong sense of family, sometimes because the church consists primarily of people related to one another by blood and matrimony. However, fellowship around the table often plays a part as well. The strongest of these churches have breakfast together every Sunday! Among the piles of pancakes, bacon, sausage, biscuits and gravy, relational bonds are formed that are not easily broken. Openness develops around the breakfast table that provides a warm environment for the worship, prayer, Bible study, and service that follows.

The fellowship that forms around the table in these country churches is about far more than food. These people really care for one another! At one church where I served as interim pastor, I would occasionally receive a call that a member had been hospitalized. I lived about a five minute drive from the hospital, and would leave home as soon as possible after I received the call. However, by the time I arrived, five or six church members were already there, ministering, encouraging, serving, and praying. Quite frankly, they were doing much better caring for one another than I could do. But they always said, "Glad you came preacher." On these occasions I often thought, "This is true fellowship. This is what church ought to be: lifting up and helping one another in time of need."

The table fellowship that takes place in small churches is often replicated in small groups that form larger congregations.

This may take a variety of forms: from a prayer group that meets for breakfast in a coffee shop, to a Bible study group that meets over lunch in cafe, to a group of families that has a backyard cookout on Saturday evening. As people break meat and bread together, they tend to open up to one another about their lives. They share stories, both about God's blessings and their personal struggles. These stories lead to opportunities to encourage one another through prayer, Bible study applied to daily living, and service to meet one another's needs. This shared life together creates a spiritual greenhouse where those seeking to grow to spiritual maturity can flourish.

This small group interaction allows for a sense of family to emerge. *Family* is not something that takes place for an hour a week at a predetermined meeting time. People participate in a family 24 hours a day, seven days a week, when they are awake or asleep, at work or at play. A church is about more than some type of small group structure. It must include the kind of support members give one another, in good times and bad, in both sickness and health (Gibbs & Bolger, 2005, pp. 97-98). Family groups do not have to follow a regular schedule: they can meet at irregular times and places in whatever way meets the needs of participants (pp. 102-03). But they do have to care for one another through prayer, sharing quality time and material resources, and service in time of need.

Life Together

"We live in a culture of shallow relationships" (Harrington & Patrick, 2017, p. 71). While we may have a "thousand friends on Facebook or Instagram," our sense of connectedness with others tends to be loose and "vulnerable" (p. 71). The only remedy for this situation is the discipleship that flows out of "shared life with others" (p. 73). "Close, enduring relationships" are essential if we going to help one another "struggle with addictions, marriage problems, living as celibate singles, or overcoming habits of indwelling sin." We must find ways to free up time in our busy schedules in order to "intentionally develop relationships" (Harrington & Patrick, 2017, p. 74).

Providing for those in need includes more than meeting physical, psychological and social needs. It also includes spiritual direction. Some refer to this as, "speaking into a person's heart": sharing words that make a heart connection with the other person, creating a spiritual bond that goes beyond intellectual instruction. We might also refer to this as, "teaching in a timely manner," or, "just the right time instruction." In any group of more than five people, there are a variety of issues. People need encouragement to dig into the Scriptures in a way that gives them the sustenance they need to meet their spiritual hunger. A person struggling in the area of prayer ought to be given instruction in the area of prayer; not training in financial management. A couple struggling with how to deal with a rebellious child needs to be counseled and taught from the Scriptures about childrearing. They are not prepared at that time, psychologically or emotionally, to endure a unit on biblical stewardship.

We must go beyond a "one size fits all" approach to biblical instruction in our disciple-making. The vast majority of discipleship today is done on the basis of books that are written to help readers understand and apply the Scriptures. The predominant discipleship method is for a group to study a book together. This is fine, as long as everyone in the group is dealing with the issues the book addresses. This may work for a time for a small group, but it does not work for a large congregation.

In order to meet spiritual needs on a timely basis, we must move beyond a typical small group structure to provide mentors who have expertise in specific areas. These mentors can provide discipleship in their area of strength to two or three people at a time through mentoring groups. Prayer warriors can provide training in prayer. Bible teachers can train in biblical interpretation. Those who lead ministries to families or to the homeless can train others to serve in these areas. This is accomplished through a combination of biblical and practical instruction, discussion of issues, and encouragement of personal application in a way that brings about life change.

Rather than inflexibly following a predetermined curriculum, trainers learn to fit their instruction to the needs of those they are discipling. This approach is flexible, timely and temporary. The discipler and those she is training covenant to meet together for *as long as needed* to accomplish their training goals. When the training need is met, the group of two to four disperses and everyone moves on to new groups and new commitments.

In a small church, people with specialized expertise may be well known in their congregation. In larger congregations, a list of mentors with contact information can be developed and dispersed, both in print and online, for those seeking growth in specific areas. Church leadership should encourage small group leaders to continue their spiritual development through this mentoring process. Group leaders can recommend mentors they know to other members of their small groups as well. This combination of mentoring groups, in combination with small groups and accountability groups, may become another piece of the fabric that makes up the disciple-making webs described in chapter five.

"Interdependence" is based on the biblical teaching that believers in the early church in Jerusalem "held all things in common" (Acts 2:44; 4:32). Randy Frazee (2001) notes that this does not mean they gave up personal property ownership.

Rather, they willingly shared what they possessed "so that those in need would be cared for" (pp. 187-88). In order to accomplish this in our day we must consider all resources—including "money, possessions, time, and talents"—to be God's resources, and then determine how he would have us use them for the good of others (p. 191). We place higher priority on caring for others than we do our own happiness (p. 199). This may mean laying aside some of our personal desires for the good of others: such as the job we do, where we live, and the lifestyle we maintain (pp. 203-08). Saying "no" to our own desires allows us to reach out in generosity to meet the needs of others (pp. 224-25).

The men in a church heard that a man in their community had developed cancer. While the cancer was treatable, the man would be out of work for two months. With very limited means, there was no way this man and his family could survive if he did not work. They gathered the church together for prayer and asked members what they could give. Although the man and his family were not church members, they were considered "neighbors," a part of the community. During the man's recovery period, church members provided "from their own pockets . . . groceries, mortgage money, meals, and other tangible support." (O'Brien, 2010, p. 69)

Interdependence is only possible to the degree that people *trust* one another. Trust develops as we "open channels of communication" (Mayers, 1974, p. 7). There is "increased sensitivity" as we seek what is best for the other person (p. 8). This takes place when mutual support and encouragement result from finding shared "meaning" through "doing" together, "giving life away" through sharing time, and "giving love" (Easum & Bandy, 1997, p. 152). It may also grow out from "shared affinity" which "can be any interest, lifestyle, task, hobby, burden, issue, or concern that passionately bonds people together." (Easum & Bandy, 1997, p. 153) Trust, like discipleship, develops over time. It begins with "friendship" and deepens to the point of "total trust and confidence." As trust develops, people become more relaxed in one another's presence. They develop the ability to communicate, both nonverbally and verbally, and become freer to share their thoughts and feelings. This mutual trust results in "bonding," or a sense of oneness (Mayers, 1974, pp. 21-24).

Community Formation

An important aspect of community formation is *reconciliation through forgiveness*. Christ-followers are called to forgive one another and others outside the community of faith in the same way that Christ has forgiven us (Matt. 6:12-15; 18:15-22). Reconciliation breaks down the walls of sin that separate people from God and from one another. Forgiveness takes place best in an environment that encourages "open confession of sin." Those who confess sin receive encouragement to repent, to turn away from sin and more fully towards Christ through "mutual accountability" and intercessory prayer with others (Dietterich, 1998, pp. 168-71). This hardly ever takes place in the context of a whole congregation or even a small group made up of ten to twelve people. Rather, it is most effective in the context of an accountability group of three or four where confidentiality and trust are more easily maintained. However, forgiveness that takes place in the context of three or four can infect a whole congregation, a neighborhood or a city.

In the small town where I grew up, there were two grocers who through years of competition developed a strong sense of animosity towards each other. They attended the same church and worshiped together, but would not speak to each other. Until one Sunday when they decided to be reconciled. I can still remember the moment when they met in the center aisle of the church worship center, shook hands and exchanged words. It was not necessary to hear what they said; everyone knew that they had put the past behind them and moved on. The atmosphere became energized as other people began to literally run around the room, asking for forgiveness and mending broken relationships. Fractured friendships were repaired. Estranged families were restored. People who had not spoken to each other for years began to pray and work together for the good of God's kingdom.

In cities where we are surrounded by people we do not know, everyone is a stranger to someone, so the stigma of being a stranger is removed. This provides the opportunity to cross barriers, to strike up conversations with people we might meet by chance at a concert or in the store. This involves taking risks among people who might harm us. Our desire to protect our families may lead to a desire for isolation. We overcome this is isolation through a "sense of civility," greeting those we meet with a "friendly hello" and learning the names of those we meet on a regular basis. These greetings open the door for the "practice of neighborliness." This begins with small acts such as watching house of a neighbor on vacation, providing childcare for one another, running errands, and providing for the needs of the elderly and homebound (Jacobsen, 2003, pp. 138-47).

Many larger churches now realize the benefit of what small churches have practiced for a long time: multiple generations coming together for mutual encouragement and support. Multi-generational disciple-making grows out of the realization that lasting change often does not occur quickly. A missionary serving in Haiti realized that it may require three generations to "eradicate" the "dark influences" of voodoo in that culture (Little, 2015, p. 306). In American culture, it may require a similar length of time to reverse the negative influences of materialism, abuse and addictions that impact both individuals and families. Some churches are "hiring personnel whose primary responsibility is to find ways to bring generations together." (O'Brien, 2010, p. 132) In a day when interaction with extended family has become rare, young people find surrogate grandparents through fellowship with senior adults, whose sense of self-worth may be restored through these relationships (p. 133). Intergenerational fellowship does not occur automatically simply because children, youth, median adults, and senior adults gather in the same room. Youth and senior adults must be brought together intentionally in shared activities such as Bible studies and service projects. And all age groups should be encouraged to read and discuss Bible stories, do art projects, garden, and participate in recreation together (pp. 134-36).

What Church Families Taught Me about Discipleship

When I was a university student I attended a medium-sized neighborhood church. I chose this church for a number of reasons. First, my older brother attended this church. Second, some guys in my dorm went to this church and since I didn't have a car, this insured that I could usually get a ride to church.

Third, I had felt a bit overwhelmed by some of the larger, city churches I visited, but this neighborhood church was only a little larger than the small town church I grew up attending, so I was comfortable. Fourth, the church had good small group Bible studies and good preaching. Looking back, it is remarkable how many of the factors in my decision of which church to attend were relational. Preaching and Bible study did factor in, but they were way down the list. If the other factors had not been in place, I probably would have never considered these theological issues.

One of the highlights of my experience at this church was participation in their family adoption ministry for students. I was "adopted" by three families. One year I was adopted a young couple: a graduate student in chemistry and his wife. Another year, it was a couple in mid-life with elementary school aged children. The third year, I became a part of the family of a senior adult couple. The primary feature of this ministry was the invitation to eat dinner with my adopted family about once a month. This was a much needed reprieve from dorm food and allowed participation in real family conversations with someone other than 18 to 21 year-olds around the dinner table. Through this experience, I was reminded that there was a "real world" a few blocks from the college campus where people worked, went to school, did household chores, and played together as families. This stretched me far beyond what I learned in the university classroom and did as much as anything to prepare me for life after college.

The students who participated in this ministry moved from the fringe to participation in the life of the church. We went from being strangers from points scattered across the United States to servants engaged in various church ministries. Some students became leaders in the church's ministries to children and youth. Others took on key roles in worship through participation in choir and hand bell choir. Over time, this church sent out many university graduates to serve, both in the church and the world. This includes pastors, worship leaders, youth and children's workers, and missionaries, as well as lawyers, educators, healthcare workers, and business leaders. A key element in these students' preparation for life was the church's investment in them through the lives of families.

It was through the ministry of this church that I experienced a calling to cross-cultural ministry. This calling has continued to provide a sense of trajectory: both where I have come from and where I am going. I doubt I would have reached my present place of service, training university students for cross-cultural ministry, were it not for discussions around the dinner table with church family members who became Christ's voice to guide me through the distractions university life and provide a foundation for a life dedicated to Christ's service.

Call to Action

- **What is your favorite food for fellowship meals?**
- **How do you move a fellowship meal from food driven to relationship driven?**
- **What do you, your group and your church need to share more of in order to develop deeper community?**
- **What relationships do you need to reconcile? What steps can you take towards reconciliation and forgiveness?**
- **What steps can your small group and/or church take to develop a greater sense of family?**

Chapter Nine

Serving Others

Serving Communities

Life in community (*koinonia*) begins with serving one another. How Christ-followers "share life together" bears witness to the surrounding community of the difference life in Christ makes (Barrett, 1998, pp. 128-29). We do this when we "share the work of Jesus" by calling people to follow him, teaching people his ways, and carrying out ministries that bring about social, psychological and physical healing (pp. 133-34). Service is the means a congregation uses to extend its reach into its community, whether this is a neighborhood, a network of families, people of the same ethnicity, culture or social class, or people who share the same vocation or hobby. To be effective in service, a church does not have to do everything. Rather, it may focus on means of service that fit the passions and giftings of the members or that meet the needs of the surrounding community. Service based on this type of congregational fit will be both unique and effective (O'Brien, 2010, pp. 88-92).

Those who reach out in service to their communities bear witness through their actions that they have been and are being transformed by God's Spirit to become more like Christ.

Meeting "felt needs" leads to the opportunity to meet deeper spiritual needs (Perkins, 1982, p. 64). While attempting to live in this way is stressful, that is what "taking up the cross and following Jesus is all about" (Luke 9:23; Gibbs & Bolger, 2005, p. 145). In the post-Christian West we must move beyond the "harvest mentality," based on evangelism that simply reaps the fruit of seed planted in good soil. "The soil is dead." It must be "rejuvenated" by pouring our lives into people so that one day an abundant harvest will come (pp. 147-48). Individuals can be changed through faith in Christ to produce a changed community. But this takes time. This does not take place when we only engage in occasional acts of service. Rather, it results when Christ-followers *live as servants* among the needy.

It is a matter of lifestyle. Serving lifestyles result from what Brandon O'Brien (2010) refers to as "high accountability/low control ministries." In these ministries, church members serve both inside and outside of the church on the basis of relationships. God works through their interests to meet the needs of others. Church staff offer encouragement, support and needed training, but they do not control these ministries (pp. 107-10). For this to occur, pastors must "relinquish control of the church's mission into the congregation's hands" (O'Brien, 2010, p. 115).

Serving Others through Prayer

A few years ago in Japan, my wife and I were attending the funeral of the grandmother of a dear friend. The funeral was Buddhist and it was customary to bow to the body of the deceased to show reverence. Many Japanese interpret this as an act of worship to the spirit of the dead. This was troubling for us because we did not want to cause any confusion. On the one hand, my wife and I wanted to be clear that we respected the person who had passed away and her family. On the other hand, we also wanted to be clear that we only worship Jesus Christ. When we reached the critical time, standing before the coffin and the family, we said, "We worship Jesus Christ. Can we pray to the God we worship for you?" The family gratefully answered, "Yes! Please pray for us!" In this way, we were able to bring encouragement to a family while bearing witness for Christ in the context of a Buddhist funeral.

For Christ-followers, prayer for others in their time of need is one of our greatest means of service. Sometimes talking to God about people is more important than "talking to people about God" (McCallum & Lowery, 2006, p. 132). Love for people, which causes us to want more for others than we are able to deliver by ourselves, will drive us to prayer (Foster, 1978, p. 40). In the case of other believers, prayer may be an automatic response. However, even when I have asked nonbelievers if I can pray for them, the answer is almost always, "Yes." Even when they are personally uncertain about God's existence or even worship another god, they may be willing to take a chance on having us pray for them in their time of need. When we pray for others, God's "life and power can flow through us" to them (Foster, 1978, p. 38). When God helps them—through encouragement, meeting a financial need, or providing healing—they can take another step in their journey towards trust in him.

Jesus provides a model prayer for his followers (Matt. 6:9-13) and often prays with them. Perhaps the most notable example was when Jesus takes his disciples to Gethsemane to pray prior to his arrest (Matt. 26:36-46; Mark 14:31-42; Luke 22:39-46). At this time more than any other, Jesus models struggling in prayer in order to submit to the Father's will. "His prayers reveal a deep, intimate relationship with God that sprang from countless hours in fellowship" (Hardin, 2009, pp. 34-35, 37). Intimate time spent with God in prayer leads to repentance and faith, which unleashes God's Spirit to "break defenses" of those who "harden their hearts" to the Gospel. This may be the beginning of "spiritual awakening" in a church, community or city (Shaw, 2014, pp. 116-17). As Christ-followers learn to pray, our thoughts and actions align with God's purposes so that God changes the world through our prayers (Foster, 1978, p. 35).

Not only is prayer *for* those in need helpful. Prayer *with* them also may demonstrate caring concern. When I meet someone in need of prayer, I often ask, "Can I pray for you *now?*" If the person assents, I try to touch them physically in some way, either by holding the person's hand or by placing one of my hands on the person's shoulder. Then I pray briefly for the person's need—no more than two or three minutes. I always complete this prayer by giving thanks to God for his faithfulness. Invariably, the people I pray for thank me and many return later to inform me of how God has answered this prayer.

Prayer also is a means small groups may use to serve people both inside and outside of their group. This may take the form of intercession for needs shared at group meetings. Or it may mean praying directly for an individual that has asked for prayer. This could take the form of praying for someone over a cup of coffee or at lunch. Or it might mean calling a group together for an extended time of intercession for a person that has physical, financial, psychological, or spiritual needs. In many small groups, the person in need is seated in the center. Others gather around placing a hand on the person's head or shoulder to show solidarity and support. Then each participant prays as they feel led by God's Spirit. When group prayer concludes with a time of thanksgiving, it teaches participants that they should not take God's blessings for granted. This results in a change of perspective from "self-centeredness" to God-centeredness (McCallum & Lowery, 2006, pp. 128-29).

Praying *with* others, either in pairs or in small groups has the added benefit of helping others learn how to pray. While people can learn about prayer through study, they learn more about prayer by watching others pray and by following their example. Prayer does not always come easily. Prayer is work and we must carry out this work of praying for others whether we feel like it or not (Foster, 1978, p. 45). When modeling for others, "frequent, shorter prayers are better than infrequent, longer prayers." People learn more when they hear us praying "simply, honestly, and personally" rather than "complicated, theological, or long" (McCallum & Lowery, 2006, p. 123). When we end our conversations in prayer we encourage those we pray for to become people who pray (Thrasher, 2003, p. 72).

Social media provides other possible avenues for sharing requests and praying for those in need. While social media is less personal than face-to-face conversation, it has the advantage of more immediate response. A person in crisis can share a need which will be shared by others through their friend networks so that people around the world can be lifting the need up in prayer within moments. Since information shared by social media is public, care must be taken to protect private information from public scrutiny. This may include eliminating the use of names and other intimate details that could be harmful if they were known publicly. While it is human nature to want to know more, our care for the well-being of those we are praying for takes precedence over our desire for information. What is most important is that the Lord knows the most intimate details of people we lift up before him. Our role in prayer is simply to place the support and well-being of people in God's hands.

Serving Others through Support

Another form of service is providing *support* through interpersonal relations. This is needed in the contemporary urban environment where "social mobility" often leads to "isolation." As people move from place to place in pursuit of a higher standard of living they often leave behind needed connections with family and friends. People in the suburbs sometimes live in fear, isolated behind locked front doors. The desire to accumulate things becomes an inadequate replacement for meaningful relationships (Block, Brueggemann & McKnight, 2016, pp. 40-41). Intergenerational isolation leads to young people creating their own "families" in the form of gangs. When these gangs have trouble making their voices heard they may turn to guns. The answer is not to focus on stopping the violence, but rather in developing the right kind of neighborhoods to raise children (pp. 42-43).

What is needed is "support persons" who will provide "stable environments" where people can reach their full potential (Mayers, 1974, pp. 268-69). This involves setting and meeting goals in a timely manner. Short-term goals must fit with long-term goals (pp. 269-71). The supporter provides "evaluation," "feedback," and "good counsel," helping the other person to grow towards "personal responsibility" (pp. 273-75). The objective is to enable a person to move beyond following instructions to develop "creative expression" using his or her own interests, gifts and abilities. A creative person develops "courage, curiosity, dedication, and a willingness to work" on a problem long-term until it is solved (Mayers, 1974, pp. 278-79).

This is most effective when it takes place in the context of communities where multiple individuals offer support. In one neighborhood people were asked what they could teach. On average, people mentioned four things they could teach others, such as "motorcycle repair, fishing and cooking." With an average of two adults per household, on a block with thirty houses, there would be 240 areas of expertise (Block, Brueggemann & McKnight, 2016, p. 53). The next block would offer another 240, and so on. Even with some overlap from house to house and block to block, many teaching possibilities would be available. These could be offered as community education courses at a local school, community center or church with two results. First, people who receive training develop better rounded, more productive lives. This productivity leads to greater confidence. Second, community interaction overcomes individual isolation. Neighbors get to know each other. Trust develops. A community of caring concern takes over. "Safe spaces" develop where people who have suffered abuse and exploitation can experience "healing" through "reconnection" with others (Gibbs & Bolger, 2005, p. 121). Within this community, the Gospel spreads through conversations about Jesus.

Serving Others through Baptism

Baptism bears witness that the Gospel changes lives. A person "buried in baptism" is raised to "walk a new life" in Christ (Rom. 6:4). When I lived in Japan, I had multiple opportunities to baptize new believers. In many Japanese churches, the person receiving baptism shares her or his testimony of how she or he came to faith in Christ. On one occasion when I was baptizing a new believer, I noticed a man standing at the back of the room that I had not seen before. He appeared to be Japanese, so I assumed he was a friend of the woman I was baptizing. I was surprised at the end of the service when the man approached me and exclaimed in perfect English,

"Now I get it! I finally get what following Christ is about!" It turns out that the man was a Japanese American, raised in Hawaii, educated in Oregon, who had come to our city on business. A church member met him and invited him to worship with us. Not having anything better to do, and perhaps with a sense of curiosity about Christianity in Japan, he showed. Through *hearing* the woman's testimony and *seeing* her baptism, he understood what it meant to follow Christ. He soon became a Christ-follower as well. Through baptism Jesus is honored, the new believer is encouraged, the church is strengthened, and those outside the fellowship of faith are drawn in.

Baptism is an outward statement of *faith,* that a person has entrusted his or her salvation to Christ's work accomplished through his death, burial and resurrection (Rom. 6:3-5; Brown, 1987, p. 105). The internal working of the Holy Spirit rather than the external act of baptism makes a person a Christ-follower. In Acts, although the sequence varies at Pentecost (2:38), Samaria (8:18-19), and the household of Cornelius (10:44-48), it is clear that baptism accompanies the Spirit's saving work (Moody, 1991, pp. 45-47). A true Christ-follower is a person who, through faith in Christ, lives under the leadership of the Holy Spirit. Baptism is an external outworking of this faith. It is possible to receive baptism in water without faith in

Christ, but baptism cannot save (Dunn, 1970, pp. 228-29). Faith is essential; baptism is secondary. Faith saves; baptism bears testimony to the world of saving faith (Brown, 1987, p. 106).

Because of this connection, some care should be taken when determining whom to baptize. We should be careful about creating a "mandatory waiting period" that may have the negative consequence of disconnecting trust in Christ from baptism. On the other hand, "an emphasis should be placed on waiting to see clear evidences of commitment and change" (Ott & Wilson, 2011, p. 230). Anecdotal evidence suggests that a majority of children brought up attending church who make professions of faith and receive baptism under age ten will repeat the process during their teen years. The rationale usually given for this phenomenon is a lack of understanding at the younger age. Those who receive re-baptism make statements like: "I really didn't understand what it meant to follow Christ," or, "I didn't know what faith in Christ meant. I really began to follow Christ when I was in high school." Pressure from family, Bible teachers and peers is the most common factor leading to these premature baptisms.

There are two necessary responses to this situation. First, we must evaluate the preparation of children to receive baptism on an individual basis. While many small children lack the degree of understanding necessary to make this step, there are others who are ready. My son, Kevin, is a case in point. When his older sister received baptism, Kevin came to me and said he was ready as well. My immediate, knee-jerk reaction was that Kevin, who was only five or six at the time, was simply following his older sister's example and really did not understand what it meant to follow Christ. When I finally agreed to baptize him a year later, Kevin said to me, "You shouldn't have made me wait. I knew what I was doing a year ago." I made a poor judgement and if I had taken the time to discuss the matter in detail with Kevin when he first came to me I wouldn't have made him wait.

Second, we need the category of *seeker* for both children and adults who make a step towards Christ, but are not ready to make a commitment to follow him. Many people make the decision to *seek* Christ before they decide to *follow* him. At this point, they may need more information, they may have doubts and questions that need to be dealt with, they may have difficulty turning away from their old way of life, or they may simply lack the will to say, "Yes," to following Christ. Whatever their issue may be, we need to affirm their decision to seek Christ without confusing them by baptizing them prematurely. I am convinced that there are many people within churches who have been baptized too soon, who continue to seek Christ, but have never really made a commitment to follow him. When this is the case and they finally make the decision to follow Christ, they may seek re-baptism as a fresh statement of their saving faith. Let us be clear that such baptism is *not* necessary for salvation because faith saves not baptism. However, these subsequent baptisms are allowable as a means of encouraging spiritual growth.

Since baptism is a proclamation of newfound faith, it should be as public as possible. There are no doubt instances where baptism is "countercultural" (Garrett, 1995, p. 536). In places where Christ-followers suffer severe persecution, there may be no choice but to baptize privately in a bath tub or a pond in a remote area. But when baptism has the "sanction of culture" (Garrett, 1995, p. 536), it should be as public as possible. While church baptisteries are not inappropriate for these occasions more public venues such as swimming pools, rivers, lakes, or the seaside are preferable. This allows the baptismal recipient to bear witness to the world: "My life has been changed. I have turned away from my old way of life. I have begun a new life as a follower of Jesus Christ." For many new Christ-followers, baptism is their initial act of *obedience* to Christ. Jesus commanded his followers to baptize those who believe as an initial step in disciple-making (Matt. 28:19; Mark 16:16). Also, Jesus provided an example through his own baptism (Matt.

3:13-17; Luke 3:21-22). Those who accept Jesus' Lordship should take advantage of this opportunity to obey him (Brown, 1987, pp. 104-05).

In many churches, only pastors or priests can baptize. These church leaders are both the intermediaries of God's grace and doorkeepers of Christ's church. Through the act of baptizing the church leader declares the recipient's faith is adequate for salvation and allows the person to participate fully in the church. This seems to be supported by at least two Scriptures. One is Matthew 16:19, in which Jesus gives his disciples the "keys of the kingdom," the authority to "bind" and "loose," both in heaven and on earth. The second is John 20:23, in which Jesus gives his disciples the authority to "forgive sins." These two passages can be interpreted to suggest that church leaders have the authority to determine the validity of a person's faith in Christ and thus forgiveness of sins.

The problem with this interpretation of Scripture is that neither of these passages explicitly mentions pastors or priests. So unless we interpret church leadership to have special sanction as successors of the apostles (the traditional Catholic view rejected by most Protestants), we should interpret these Scriptures to mean that every Christ-follower holds the kingdom keys and every believer has the ability to offer the forgiveness of sins available through faith in Christ. So every baptized disciple should be able to baptize others. While many churches have maintained the tradition that only pastors and priests can baptize, many other churches have taken the step of allowing other believers to baptize as well. While the most common practice is allowing other men, such as fathers, deacons or small group leaders, to baptize those under their leadership, some churches also allow women to baptize others. Some argue that there is no biblical example of a woman baptizing, but there is no explicit prohibition against it either. For the purpose of disciple-making, it is most natural for the person who leads a person to faith in Christ to baptize the new believer. In most cases this will result in: parents baptizing their children; group leaders baptizing participants in their groups; men baptizing men; and women baptizing women. Every Christ-follower has an equal stake, and equal responsibility, in carrying out the Great Commission (Matt. 28:16-20). Baptism should take place within the relational contexts of small groups and disciple-making webs where most spiritual growth occurs.

Baptism enables us to participate in a community of those formerly separated from one another by ethnicity, culture, religion, social status, and gender (Gal. 3:27-28; Brown, 1987, pp. 106-07). This is particularly important for people who come to faith in Christ out of other religious backgrounds such as Muslims or Hindus. In this case, those who once experienced a "wall of separation" from Christ and his people have now been joined together in Christ (Eph. 2:14), only to find the wall reconstructed in another location. Connection with a Christian community may have a "significant impact on the disciple's relationship to his or her family, friends, and former community of faith" (Ott & Wilson, 2011, p. 231). The good news is that through baptism previously "isolated individuals" become a community of mutually affirming "brothers and sisters." Believers linked together by love learn to follow Christ by laying down their lives to meet the needs of others (Dietterich, 1998, p. 161).

Acts of Kindness Change Lives

Some believe that only acts of service carried out on a grand scale have lasting value. They think "big picture," like a citywide blood drive, a food and clothes closet to care for the needs of neighborhood poor, or a daily soup kitchen that feeds the homeless in the inner-city. While it is true that these long-term projects have the capacity to bring about lasting change, we should not overlook the possibility of changing lives through small acts of kindness. The Bible reveals that even small acts that meet needs have the power to change the world. A cup of water served by the woman at the well gave everyone in Sychar the opportunity to come to faith in Christ (John 4:10-11, 40-42). The offer of a stable to Joseph and Mary provided the birthplace for the Savior of the world (Luke 2:7-12). Sharing the contents of a lunch box allowed Jesus to feed over five thousand people (John 6:1-10). And providing a burial place set the stage for Jesus' defeat of death through his resurrection from the dead (John 19:38; Matt. 28:1-6; Luke 24:1-6).

While acts of kindness we provide and receive on a daily basis do not bring about such dramatic results as feeding a multitude and raising the dead, they do change lives. Yesterday, I pulled into my drive at the end of a long day of work, noticed my overgrown lawn, and wondered when I might get around to cutting the grass. Just then, I noticed my neighbor cutting across his front yard to meet me at my car door. Before I even had time to get out of my car he asked, "Would you mind if I mowed your lawn?" Being an able-bodied, middle-aged, American male with some sense of pride and self-sufficiency, my immediate response was, "That really isn't necessary." But my neighbor insisted, "I know, but I have a big riding lawnmower and you just have that little push mower. I want to help." Almost before I knew what I was saying, I heard the words, "Yes, that would be great." Issue settled. My lawn was mowed, and I moved on to other weighty matters. This act of kindness has not changed anyone's eternity, yet. But I have been wondering how to get to know this neighbor who recently moved from California to help his aging parents. Other than saying, "Hi," I haven't figured out how to converse with him, much less talk about spiritual matters. It seems like God may be providing a crack in a closed door.

Later this afternoon, I am baking a pan of frozen lasagna for a group of young people that come from dysfunctional homes that meets at my church on Wednesday nights. There really is not much to buying a frozen lasagna from the freezer section at the local market and then putting it into the oven for a couple of hours. But when put together with other pasta, bread, salad, and dessert that my small group at church is providing, it may provide the opportunity for conversations of eternal significance around the dinner table.

Acts of kindness can be transformational, whether we are helping others or receiving their help. Our needs enable "people to accept us as part of them" (Perkins, 1982, p. 61). When we take a "position to receive," we open both ourselves and others up to "God's provision" (p. 62). Jesus received both a cup of cold water and a boy's lunch. He used these acts of service as opportunities to share God's grace. Whether we are giving or receiving acts of kindness, these events become opportunities to share our human frailty with others. Shared weakness becomes the bridge over which God's grace passes from Christ-followers to seekers. Through our common frailty we discover trust in one another that leads us to trust in Christ together.

Very often joint projects can be carried out based on "shared values" between Christ-followers and nonbelievers who live around them. Church members may either launch new initiatives or simply join ongoing neighborhood projects (Frost & Hirsch, 2003, p. 25). Watching small children so their parents can participate in counseling may save a marriage. Buying a small gift for a depressed friend may save her from suicide. A car repair may help a person get to an interview, leading to a job, enabling a family to overt economic hardship. Coaching a student through a difficult mathematical concept may enable an aspiring student to take the next step towards becoming a doctor who discovers a cure for cancer.

Call to Action

- Who do you need to pray for?
- How can your small group strengthen your service through intercessory prayer?
- Who could you serve through words or acts of encouragement?
- Who needs to take next step of following Christ through baptism? How could you encourage him or her?
- What small act of kindness could you do today?

Chapter Ten
Transforming Communities

In the context of the world's cities, a variety of churches have a role to play in the disciple-making process: from mega-churches to micro-churches; from inner-city churches to neighborhood churches; and from ethnic churches to churches built around common interests. The size, location and constituency of these churches impact *who* they disciple. Other issues impact *how* disciple-making is done and to what degree their process is effective. Many people in Western culture are "fascinated by spirituality, and yet remarkably ignorant of Christianity." They are "hostile to organized religion," yet yearn for spiritual wholeness (Easum & Bandy, 1997, p. 28). How does the church *fit* its community in a way that transforms these people into committed Christ-followers? How does the church serve this community? How does it go about fellowship, worship and witness? And how are outsiders drawn into the web of relationships in which disciple-making takes place?

One semester at Southwest Baptist University, I was nearing the end of teaching a disciple-making course. We had discussed the role of churches and small groups in the formation of Christ-followers. I had emphasized that disciple-making is most effective in the context of local churches where believers can encourage one another to grow towards Christlikeness. Then a student raised his hand and said, "What you are saying sounds wonderful, but is it realistic? If you are describing what a church should be like, then I have never been part of a real church. Are there any churches that work together to make disciples? Or is this just wishful thinking?"

This book is an attempt to answer questions my student and others raise about the role of local churches in making disciples. Christ-followers have a biblical mandate to make disciples among the nations (Matt. 28:16-20). But, as we have seen from history, sometimes we have made "Christians" who are not committed Christ-followers. In response to this issue, we must find ways to encourage those who live on the margins of Christian communities to move towards total commitment to follow Christ. Martin Robinson and Dwight Smith (2003) remind us that,

> Those who live in our community are significantly influenced by whether or not the church has social value. . . . The way in which we live and bear witness significantly influences the view that the wider community has of the church. (p. 60)

Jesus commanded us to make disciples, and we have some idea of what this should look like. We really want to be growing disciples who make disciples. But there is a gap between our knowledge and our performance. How we should live and how we actually live are not the same. How do we close this gap between "talking the talk" and "walking the walk"? How can isolated individuals, small groups and churches *begin* the task of making disciples in our communities? In this final chapter, I want to make a number of suggestions to help you and your friends get started along the path towards building a church that will make disciples in your community.

Get Out of Your House

If we are going to make disciples in our communities, we must begin by getting off the couch and walking out of our front door. This may seem too simplistic, but how long has it been since you have actually taken a walk in your neighborhood? Thankfully, some of us do this almost daily, but for many others the answer to this question is either, "Much too long," or, "I never have." Until we get out of the house into the neighborhood, we will never really find out what our community is like. Unless we know what our community is like, we do not know what changes need to be made. Until we understand what changes need to be made, we cannot bring about needed community transformation. We may have some good ideas, but we will never verify whether these thoughts fit the real world we live in.

Some may respond, "I can see enough through the window. I don't need to go outside." The problem with this fortress mentality is that, while keeping our families safe the walls of our houses may prevent us from interacting with others. Unless we risk getting to know people we will never be able to help them. The people we meet in today's cities are often overwhelmed by "complex social relationships," "multiple tasks" that result in feelings of "fragmentation," rapid change that makes it hard to keep up, and "radical forms of individuality producing isolation and aloneness" (Van Gelder, 1998, p. 20). Endless "technological choices," "transient relationships," and the over-individualization of spirituality and social norms has resulted in a loss of cohesion (pp. 37-39). This erosion of community has made "individualism" a "forced condition" rather than a personal "choice." People who long for relationships with others often find themselves very much alone (p. 43).

One of my customs is to walk from my house to the central business district of the town I live in, Bolivar, Missouri. Bolivar is more of a small town than a city, so this walk only requires about twenty minutes. Perhaps my urge to walk is a holdover from living in Tokyo where, almost every day, my family and I walked from our house to the shopping district near our local train station. In Tokyo there were many walkers. In Bolivar there are almost none. A friend in Bolivar once cautioned me, "Don't walk the streets; there are crazy people living here!" But as of the writing of this book, I have survived the dangers of Bolivar's streets.

Others may respond, "I may not know *what* the people in my community need, but I know *who* they need: they need *Jesus!*" While this is no doubt true, we will never have the opportunity to talk with people about Jesus unless we go *where they are*. It is unlikely that our neighbors are going to show up at our front door asking us to tell them about Jesus. This is true, whether we are talking about the door of our houses or the doors of our churches. We must enter into our community's life to experience "its rhythm and its people from the inside" (Frost & Hirsch, 2003, p. 39). We must meet people in their natural element. We must engage them where they live life: in the workplace and the marketplace; in schools and on playgrounds; in places of both suffering and healing. Otherwise, they will never know that Jesus loves them.

Show You Care

It often has been said, "People don't care what we say until they know that we care." We show that we care through serving others. Service takes on many forms, large and small. Our service may be as small as providing dinner for a family with a sick family member, or as large as organizing a soup kitchen to feed the homeless. It may be as small as mowing a neighbor's lawn, or as large as organizing a group of volunteers to clean the neighborhood park. It may be as small as adding a few items to our shopping cart for our neighbor, or as large as organizing a food closet. It may be as small babysitting so the couple next door can have a date night, or as large as developing an afterschool program to help neighborhood children learn how to read.

As much as we want to solve everyone's problems, there are some situations that we cannot fix. John MacArthur tells the story of being called to help at a home where a baby had just died. When MacArthur entered the home, a distraught mother took him to the bedroom where an infant girl, three or four months, lie dead on a bed. The mother and later paramedics tried to revive the child, but to no avail (MacArthur, 1991, p. 166). The attempt to "fix" every situation can result in a sense of "futility." It is tempting to see the people we are called to serve as begging us to fix their lives when what they really want is to know we love them (Smith, 2008, pp. 111-12). What can we say to a weeping mother who has just lost her child? Sometimes there are no words that will bring comfort. All we can do is hold her hand, weep with her, and pray for God's comfort.

Our primary example of service is Jesus who washed his disciples' feet (John 13:3-17). Jesus said, "If I then, the Lord and the Teacher, washed your feet, you also ought to wash one another's feet. For I gave you an example that you also should do as I did to you" (John 13:14-15). Sometimes during an ordination service, the feet of newly ordained pastors and deacons are washed as a symbol of the life of service they are beginning. As moving as it is to observe "foot washing" in these contexts, this really does not approach what Jesus did for his disciples. Jesus did not wash his disciples' feet merely as a symbol of how they should serve one another. Jesus washed their feet as a real act of service! The streets of Jerusalem were littered not only with dirt, but also with animal dung as well. As a result of walking those streets wearing sandals, the disciples' feet were filthy. So filthy in fact that no one wanted to clean them. Washing feet was a servant's job, but no servant in the house wanted to wash those feet. Jesus took on a thankless job that no one else was willing to do.

Tasks that no one does usually are *not* overlooked tasks. They are tasks that everyone is aware of, but no one wants to do. We must be willing to do what it takes to make a difference—to take time, to sweat, and to get dirty when necessary. There will be some inconvenience and effort. We may not enjoy our labor, but the results will be worth it. The dirty are made clean; the hungry are fed; the discouraged are encouraged; the homeless have a warm room with a bed; the neighborhood park becomes a safe place for children to play. When we act in Christ-like service, Jesus works through us to "confer grace" on the suffering. Our deeds "reveal God in his goodness" (Frost & Hirsch, 2003, p. 137). In this way, we "incarnate" the message of Christ's love in the communities where we live (pp. 146-62)

Go Public

There is a growing chorus of voices in North America shouting, "Personal spirituality is a private matter!" We are told the church should have no voice in politics. Also, people of faith, Muslims and Jews as well as Christians, are expected to keep quiet on moral issues related to family life and even the right to life. Many people do not openly reject Christianity. Rather, "they care nothing about God or spirituality" (Beshears, 2017, p. 257). So they find no value in conversations about spiritual and moral issues. They remain "indifferent" to the claims of Christianity as a way to protect their personal "autonomy" (p. 268). These secularists "intellectually suppress the truth about God's character to ease their guilt and nullify any moral obligation to him" (p. 260).

We cannot transform our neighborhoods by remaining silent. Not only must we get out of the house, we must also speak up. Christ-followers must make our voices heard on issues that matter, whether it be the rights of the unborn or providing quality care for the elderly. Both of these issues are part of the larger framework commonly referred to as the "right to life." Christian concern for life must not end with childbirth, but rather must include every level of human development such as: quality healthcare and housing, the need for childcare, education and vocational training, as well as strengthening the quality of family life.

Political and social activism is only a small part of voicing our concerns. History suggests that we will not change public opinion through the ballot box. Rather, we must seek to enter into conversations on important matters, not only with those we agree with, but also more importantly with those we are likely to with disagree with. If any progress is to be made, we must move beyond the tendency to shout past each other to re-engage in the lost art of conversation. This will only happen when those who claim to be Christ-followers follow his example of humility based on love. We are the ones who must stop shouting first; we are the ones who must begin to listen. There are no guarantees that this will work. But if Christ-followers are willing to listen long enough and loud enough, just maybe we will earn the right to be heard.

Josh Patrick tells the story of meeting a man named Scott who was skeptical about Jesus. Josh thanked Scott for his openness and said he would like to hear more of Scott's story. This led to a series of "weekly lunch meetings that continued for six months." Occasional talks about Jesus were interspersed with conversations about "sports, marriage, and careers." Eventually, this led to Scott having increased interest in Jesus, which led to his participation in a small group Bible study, which resulted in Scott placing his faith in Jesus as his Lord and Savior. Patrick notes that the journey which resulted in Scott's salvation began with Josh's willingness to invest time in him. Josh had to take the initiative for Scott to come to faith in Christ (Harrington & Patrick, 2017, pp. 111-12).

It is through our conversations with friends in coffee shops and living rooms that communities will be changed. This change will not come about as long as we only discuss human rights and the need for better schools and parks. As important as these conversations are (and they are important!), the real change that needs to come will only take place when talk about how life blends into spirituality, and how spirituality leads to conversations about and with Jesus. This Jesus talk will not come quickly, but it must come if the people who live around us are going to experience needed change. Those who do not know Jesus are looking for relationships in which they can receive the needed "support" to "struggle with the effects of sin" (Harrington & Patrick, 2017, p. 76). Make no mistake: this new life only comes through faith in Jesus Christ (John 3:16; Eph. 2:8).

Talk about Jesus

Eugene Peterson (2008) reminds us that most of our talking takes place in the context of "informal conversational give-and-take while eating meals at home or with friends, walking on the road between villages, or in response to interruptions by questions on the road to somewhere or other" (p. 13). We will only be effective in making disciples to the extent that we include Jesus in these everyday conversations. While "God talk" is a regular part of our Sunday regimen, in between we tend to engage in "small talk." Yet it is in the context of these "unstructured, informal conversations" that occur during the week at home and at work, on the playground and in the super market, while drinking iced tea or eating a meal together, that life change so often takes place (p. 14). This is because a kind of intimacy develops naturally when men and women walk and talk together, with no immediate agenda or assigned task except eventually getting to their destination and taking their time to do it. (Peterson, 2008, p. 16).

In over thirty years of preaching and teaching in churches and universities, I have noticed most significant conversations take place either between classes or after worship. Not that sermons and lessons are unimportant. When well done, they plant seeds that bring about spiritual harvest. But much of the tilling and cultivation comes in conversations that move from general principle to personal application. People struggling through life issues ask questions like, "What does this mean for me?" or, "What do I need to do?" People want to know what God wants them to do and they want to know that God cares for them. Sometimes they are not certain. We need to help them know for sure. When people "open the door to spiritual conversation," we need to "share our story about why Jesus is essential" for our lives (Easum, 2001, p. 151).

For our conversations about Jesus to be meaningful, nonbelievers must be able to understand who we say Jesus is. Peter said Jesus is "the Christ, the Son of the Living God" (Matt. 16:16). But today terms like "Christ," "Son of God," "Lord," and "Savior" require more theological knowledge than many people have (Easum & Bandy, 1997, p. 39). For many people, understanding historical Christian teaching about Christ has become less important than experiencing Christ today. Denominational traditions that divide Christ-followers has become less important than authentic faith that unites us. People yearn to experience the healing, transforming power of Jesus Christ. They want to know that Jesus will stand with them in times of trouble when they are victimized by violence and social injustice. They want to experience the unity and harmony that only Jesus can bring when the world is torn apart by strife (Easum & Bandy, 1997, 40-49). Easum and Bandy (1997) write, "There is a depth to Jesus that is unique. One does not take direction from Jesus, but one walks with Jesus into the unknown" (p. 55).

Rather than overwhelming friends by trying to share too much too quickly, we should be prepared to go slowly. Consistent investment of time in spiritual conversations leads to vulnerable sharing that results in making disciples (McCallum & Lowery, 2006, p. 72). Open conversations in which people are free to express their doubts and seek answers in a "caring non-judgmental" setting will help them find faith and forgiveness (Hunter, 1992, p. 58). This type of communication begins with "active listening" that includes "interest" and "acceptance." People "want and need to be heard" (Hunter, 1992, p. 98). When we listen, we are able to answer questions in a way that provides a "point of contact" between the "gospel and pressing human needs" (p. 100). Over a period of time, the cumulative effect of these conversations is that people learn to trust in a "multifaceted Gospel" that includes God's love and grace, forgiveness, reconciliation, new birth, and eternal life (p. 103).

Celebrate Jesus

Celebrations bring people together. Festivities provide opportunities for fun. People love to line streets for parades, to eat special foods, and to ooh and awe over fireworks. Laughter and shouts of joy fill the air. For a day at least, the commonality of shared experience supersedes differences that divide us—social class, age, gender, culture, and language. Everyone is drawn together by our common love for pageantry and spectacle. We feel caught up in the exuberance of life together!

City-wide celebrations like homecoming and the fourth of July, football games and concerts in the park, give Christ-followers opportunities to gather with family and friends, to picnic, to share stories, to play games, and to have fun. We shout greetings to friends who pass by on floats in the parade, and then cheer for our local athletic teams as they take on detested rivals. All in fun, hopefully. After all, sports are only games, not real life. But as we share emotions *together* it reminds us what it means to be really alive! At these times we can share our passion for living, that life is God's gift, and that it should be lived in a way that honors him. Oftentimes, these times of sharing give way to quiet conversations in the evening shadows: opportunities to say, "God is good. There are problems along the way, but it really is good to be alive."

In much of the world, Christmas is the most popular celebration of the year. People love to give and get gifts, to see Christmas trees, tinsel and lights, and to hear "Jingle Bells" and "Rudolph" blaring from speakers on every corner. Singing "Silent Night" is a beloved tradition, even among those who give little to no recognition of Christmas as a celebration of Christ's birth. The fact is, Christmas is only as "Christian" as Christ-followers make it. While we may disdain the materialism that has seemingly taken over the contemporary celebration, we still have the opportunity to share the story of Christ's birth in a very public way. We tend to hold concerts and plays in our houses of worship, which we advertise hoping that some who do not know Christ will show up. When the advertising and performance are elaborate enough, they do get public attention. But this may leave the impression that Jesus is for the church, not for the city.

We must find a way to take our celebrations of Jesus at Christmas outside the walls of the church building, into the streets and places where people gather throughout the community. One way this can be done is through re-initiating the historical practice of Christmas caroling. Groups of believers can sing Christmas carols where people gather—on busy streets and in shopping malls, in offices and restaurants (with the permission of the owners of course). Think "flash mob." A group suddenly gathers from nowhere to sing songs of

Jesus' birth, then just as suddenly disperses into the crowd, handing out pamphlets that describe why we celebration Christmas, including a brief biblical account of Jesus' birth.

Another possibility is Christmas parties hosted by groups of believers for unbelieving friends. A mix of half believers and half unbelievers is best. And not too many people: we don't want introverts to get lost in the crowd. We want a festive atmosphere with holiday foods, singing and games. Somewhere in the mix, someone takes a few minutes to talk about Jesus' birth in a basic, understandable way. Everyone leaves the party knowing that Christmas is about Jesus and that his birth is the reason we celebrate.

Thanksgiving is another American holiday that has great spiritual potential, especially within families. Most often these family gatherings center on food and football. But there is at least a little recognition of the historical basis for this holiday in the celebration of the Pilgrims and Native Americans at Plymouth in 1621. Families can easily extend this thought to a time of prayer, giving thanks to God for his blessings throughout the year. However, I have found that an extended time of prayer just prior to the Thanksgiving feast is impracticable. Rumbly tummies make for short prayers. What is better is a separate time later in the day, perhaps between naps and after we get bored with football. Simply gather everyone in the family room, read a psalm of thanks (such as Psalm 100), then ask everyone to share one blessing they are thankful for. Close with a brief prayer. This simple, yet powerful time of sharing and giving thanks can breathe new spiritual life into a traditional family gathering.

One other Christian celebration that provides an opportunity to make Christ known is Easter. Whereas Christmas is now celebrated for the whole month of December or even longer, in many churches the celebration of Easter is limited to a single day, or even a single morning. And many times this celebration takes place within the church with little impact on the surrounding community. This should not be the case. Easter is the celebration of the most pivotal event of human history: the resurrection of Jesus Christ. So we should develop as whole season for the celebration of Easter just as we now have for Christmas. Perhaps Lint is an attempt to do this, but Lint tends to be mournful when Easter calls for a joyous celebration. I would suggest public performances of Passion Plays, depicting the crucifixion and resurrection of Jesus Christ. It is great to present these plays in churches and invite people to come, but it would be even better if we could find more public venues to present these performances. When churches are small so they lack resources to present plays, a group of churches in a city could work together. Also, similar to the

Christmas, during the Easter season we could host home gatherings in which Lord's Supper is celebrated in the context of a fellowship meal. Along with this, there should be a brief telling of biblical story of Jesus' death and resurrection as well. This would provide a living witness to the cross and resurrection of Christ in the context of Christian community.

What of bunnies and eggs? These aspects of Easter have a pagan origin. However, I am not opposed to continuing these traditions with children as long as we make clear that there is a difference between "make believe" and "real." We need to begin to teach children at an early age that Easter is a celebration of new life, and that new life only comes to us as a gift of God's grace through faith in Jesus Christ (Eph. 2:8-9). While bunnies and eggs may symbolize new life, the true source of this life is Jesus.

The Scattered Church

Brad Smith (2008) defines the *scattered church* as "individual believers or small groups of believers in families, neighborhoods, and workplaces being the church in ways that are not organized or programmed by leaders of the church community" (p. 65). In the city, people struggle daily with life and death. The church infiltrates the city to encourage people to choose life. Not only physical life that ebbs and flows away, but also spiritual life that remains forever. David Swartz (1990) vividly illustrates this mission.

One day a man lingered on the front steps of our church until everyone was gone. He had attended occasionally, and we'd had some good talks at his apartment. Carl said he wanted to apologize. I couldn't imagine what he wanted to apologize for, so he explained.

His life had been hard. At one point it became so bad that suicide seemed to be the only escape. He attempted to hang himself but used an old rope, which snapped—but not until he'd hung for at least a minute or two, feeling that noose strangling his life away before he fell to the floor.

"That's why I want to apologize. You see, to this day I can't stand to wear a tie or button my collar. I can't stand anything tight around my neck. I hope younand your folks here weren't offended. Dave, does God understand why I can't wear a tie?"

My throat was tight but I managed to get it out, "Of course he understands if you don't wear a tie". (pp. 168-69)

Swartz (1990) writes, "Christianity only appears to be safe" (p. 38). In reality, it is a movement orchestrated by God's Spirit that infiltrates the lives of people in communities, societies, and nations with the "transforming nature of Jesus Christ" (Swartz, 1990, pp. 38-39). When we participate in this movement, we move beyond the limitations of human planning to participate in what only God can do (pp. 91-92). The Holy Spirit leads the advance beyond the borders of our comfort zone to connect with people we usually pass by: the poor and needy, the rich but needy, those caught up in sexual sins and substance abuse, and the divorced. Our "church culture" may consider these people spiritually "unclean," and we may feel "inadequate" to overcome the barriers that separate us. We must take risks if these people are to experience Christ's love (Swartz, 1990, pp. 155-65).

In order to make disciples, a gathered church must scatter beyond the walls of its meeting place, infiltrating the lives of others through shared community. This only takes place to the extent that we are intentional about going into the community, speaking the Gospel, and sharing Christ's love in both word and deed. Let us not be merely "hearers of the Word," but also "doers of the Word" (James 1:22) so that others who see us following Christ may become Christ-followers as well.

Call to Action

- What fears prevent you from leaving your house to enter into your community?
- Who can you serve and how can you serve them?
- Are there other Christ-followers that you can include in acts of service?
- What issues do you need to take a stand on?
- Who should you talk with about Jesus?
- How can you, your small group or your church celebrate Jesus *publicly* in your neighborhood or city?

Epilogue
New Beginnings

Recently, the media has inundated us with stories about people who have lost their future because of their past. Due to some misdeed, whether in their recent or distant past, many people have lost families, careers and opportunities to make the world a better place. There is a presupposition within many cultures around the world that people can *never* change. People are defined by past actions. They are on predetermined highways with no exits. Their destiny awaits. People are who they are so we must confront them and hold them accountable. Accountability is good when it challenges people to leave the past behind and move forward to a new way of life. But the current kind of accountability that tears people down and destroys their lives is not good.

In contrast with this culture of inescapable destruction, Jesus Christ brings promise of new life. Because of Jesus people do not have to be defined by their past, but rather have the opportunity to begin again. "If anyone is in Christ he is a new creature; the old things passed away, new things have come" (2 Cor. 2:17). People who turn from their old way of life are re-created through faith in Christ (2 Cor. 5:15, 21).

New beginnings are found throughout the Bible. They are so common that it is impossible to list every example, so let the following litany of names suffice. God was so grieved by the wickedness of human beings that he decided to begin again with Noah (Gen. 6-8). God called Abraham to become the father of a new nation through whom all the families of the earth would be blessed (Gen. 12:1-4). God called Moses to turn back from following Jethro's flocks in order to lead the people of Israel out of Egypt (Ex. 3-4). God called Ruth to leave Moab in order to serve him in Bethlehem (Ruth 1:16-17). As a result of Ruth's response, she became the great-grandmother of King David and an ancestor of Jesus (Ruth 4:17). David the faithful shepherd was chosen by God to become king over Israel (1 Sam. 16:11-13).

Jesus chose four fishermen (Matt. 4:18-21), a tax collector (Matt. 9:9), and seven others to become his apostles (Luke 6:13-16). Jesus was extremely patient his followers. He did not give up on them when they did not believe. Thomas doubted Jesus' resurrection until Jesus let Thomas see and touch him, then Thomas believed (John 20:25-28). Before Jesus crucifixion Peter denied that he even knew Jesus (John 18:17-27). But after his resurrection Jesus gave Peter three opportunities to declare his love for Jesus and commissioned him to care for Jesus' followers (John 21:15-19). Saul was a murderer of Christ-followers until he met Jesus on the Damascus Road. Then he became Paul, Jesus' apostle to the Gentiles (Acts 9:1-15).

In my life, I have found that while Jesus loves me as I am, he also loves me too much to leave me unchanged. Rather, he has given me multiple opportunities to begin again, each time re-creating me more completely in Christ's image. My initial re-creation came when, as a nine-year-old boy, I responded to Jesus' call to follow him. Jesus forgave my sins and gave me eternal life (Rom. 6:23). This is a wonderful story of God's saving grace, but Jesus was not finished with me yet. As a university student, I responded to Jesus' call to serve as a missionary in Japan. At this point, the Lord's Great Commission (Matt. 28:16-20) became my own. While I could not reach the whole world, I could do my part by making disciples among the Japanese. Then about 25 years later, the Lord broadened my vision, calling me to prepare students to take the Gospel to the nations through teaching at Southwest Baptist University. Through all of these new beginnings, I have grown as a Christ-follower. Even though I have followed Christ for over forty years, I am confident that Jesus is not finished with me yet: I still have a lot of spiritual growth ahead.

Churches also have the opportunity to begin again. A church which has made little impact on its community can reshape its structure and revitalize its ministries. It can begin to reach out into the surrounding neighborhood with new ministries, beginning new fellowship groups meeting in homes and offices, sharing the love of Jesus Christ with people that have been overcome by the burdens of life. Churches that for many years have only existed as relics of some bygone glory can experience new life as disciple-making communities.

In disciple-making, as long as this life continues we never reach the final chapter. There is always only new beginnings. There is always the opportunity for people to turn from sin to faith in Christ, to say "yes" to a deeper walk with him, to yield more completely to his calling in their lives, to come more clearly to resemble the image of Christ. Jesus calls us daily, and each day we take up our cross anew to follow him (Luke 9:23).

About The Author

Kelly Malone holds a Ph.D. in Theology and Missions from Southwestern Baptist Theological Seminary. Currently, he is Professor of Intercultural Studies and holds the Jack Stanton Chair of Evangelism at Southwest Baptist University, Bolivar, Missouri. In this position, he mentors and coaches students who are preparing to engage in urban ministries throughout the world. Previously, Malone served in the cities of Japan for fifteen years where he taught at a university, planted churches and trained leaders.

References

Amin, A. (2013). The urban condition: A challenge to social science. *Public culture, 25*(2), 201-08.

Bakke, R. (1984). Evangelization of the world's cities. In L. L. Rose & C. K. Hadaway (Eds.), *An urban world: Churches face the future* (pp. 75-94). Nashville: Broadman Press.

Bandy, T. G., & Holmes, L. S. (2014). *Worship ways: For the people within your reach*. Nashville: Abingdon Press.

Bare Bulb Coffee Shop closes its doors. (2016). Retrieved December 21, 2017, from   http://www.13wmaz.com/news/bare-bulb coffee   shop closes-its-doors/61919739.

Barrett, L. (1998). Missional witness: The church as apostle to the world. In D. L. Guder (Ed.), *Missional church: A vision for the sending of the church in North America* (pp. 110-41). Grand Rapids: William B. Eerdmans Publishing Company.

Beale, G, K. (2004). *The temple and the church's mission: A biblical theology of the dwelling place of God*. Downers Grove, IL: Inter Varsity Press.

Best, H. M. (2003). *Unceasing worship*. Downers Grove, IL: Inter Varsity Press.

Block, D. I. (2014). *For the glory of God: Recovering a biblical theology of worship*. Grand Rapids: Baker Academic.

Block, P., Brueggemann, W., & McKnight, J. (2016). *Another kingdom: Departing the consumer culture.*Hoboken, NJ: John Wiley & Sons.

Bloesch, D. G. (2002). *The church*. Downers Grove, IL: Inter Varsity Press.

Bosch, D. J. (1991). *Transforming mission: Paradigm shifts in theology of mission*. Maryknoll, NY: Orbis Books.

Bright, J. (1981). *A history of Israel* (3rd ed.). Philadelphia: Westminster Press.

Brofman, O., & Beckstrom, R. A. (2006). *The starfish and the spider*. New York: Portfolio.

Brown, C. (2014). Gathering neighbors: City Church of East Nashville. In M. L. Branson & N. Warnes (Eds.), *Starting missional churches* (pp. 66-85). Downers Grove, IL:IVP Books.

Brown, G. (2011). Effective cross-cultural ministry teams. In A. S. Moreau & B. Snodderly (Eds.), *Reflecting God's glory together* (pp. 141-61). Pasadena: William Carey Library.

Brown, L. D. (1987). *The life of the church*. Nashville: Broadman Press.

Calfee, R. (2013). Identifying persons of peace. In C. Crider, L. McCrary, R. Calfee, & W. Stephens (Eds.), *Tradecraft for the church on mission* (pp. 102-23). Portland, OR: Urban Loft Publishers.

Cate, R. L. (1982). *Old Testament roots for New Testament faith*. Nashville: Broadman Press.

Chan, S. (2018). *Evangelism in a skeptical world*. Grand Rapids: Zondervan Press.

Chapell, B. (2009). *Christ-centered worship*. Grand Rapids: Baker Academic.

Cherry, C. M. (2010). *The worship architect: A blueprint for designing culturally relevant and biblically faithful services*. Grand Rapids: Baker Academic.

Choung, James. (2012). *Real Life*. Downers Grove, IL: Inter-Varsity Press.

Chute, A. L., & Morgan, C. W. (2017). Missional spirituality as congregational. In N. A. Finn & K. S. Whitfield (Eds.), *Spirituality for the sent: Casting a new vision for the missional church* (pp. 75-95). Downers Grove, IL: IVP Academic.

Cole, N. (1999). *Cultivating a life for God*. St. Charles, IL: Church Smart Resources.

Cole, N. (2005). *Organic church: Growing faith where life happens*. San Francisco: Jossey-Bass.

Crawley, W. (1984). Urbanization and Christian ministry in world history. In L. L. Rose & C. K. Hadaway (Eds.), *An urban world: Churches face the future* (pp. 37-50). Nashville: Broadman Press.

Decker, M. S. (2008). Student sojourners and spiritual formation. In R. J. Priest (Ed.), *Effective engagement in short term missions: Doing it right* (pp. 558-89). Pasadena: William Carey Library.

Dietterich, I. T. (1998). Mission community: Cultivating communities of the Holy Spirit. In D. L. Guder (Ed.), *Missional church: A vision for the sending of the church in North America* (pp. 142-82). Grand Rapids: William B. Eerdmans Publishing Company.

Dillon, C. (2012). *Telling the gospel through story*. Downers Grove, IL: Inter-Varsity Press.

Drummond, L. A. (2002). *Reaching generation next*. Grand Rapids: Baker Books.

Duck, R. C. (2013). *Worship for the whole people of God*. Louisville: Westminster John Knox Press.

Dunn, J. D. G. (1970). *Baptism in the Holy Spirit*. Philadelphia: Westminster Press.

Dyrness, W. (1977). *Themes in Old Testament theology*. Downers Grove, IL: Inter-Varsity Press.

Easum, B. (2000). *Leadership on the other side*. Nashville: Abingdon Press.

Easum, B. (2001). *Unfreezing moves*. Nashville: Abingdon Press.

Easum, W. M., & Bandy, T. G. (1997). *Growing spiritual redwoods*. Nashville: Abingdon Press.

Ellison, C. W. (1997). Addressing felt needs of urban dwellers. In H. M. Conn (Ed.), *Planting and growing urban churches: From dream to reality* (pp. 94-110). Grand Rapids: Baker Books.

Engel, J. F. (1975). *Contemporary Christian communication*. Nashville: Thomas Nelson Publishers.

Engel, J. F., & Dyrness, W. A. (2000). *Changing the mind of missions: Where have we gone wrong*. Downers Grove, IL: Inter-Varsity Press.

Escobar, S. (2003). *The new global mission: The gospel from everywhere to everyone*. Downers Grove, IL: IVP Academic.

Everts, D., & Schaupp, D. (2008). *I once was lost*. Downers Grove, IL: Inter-Varsity Press.

Fielding, C. (2008). *Preach and heal: A biblical model for missions*. Richmond: International Mission Board.

First Baptist Bolivar. (2018). Retrieved January 2, 2018, from http://www.fbcbolivar.org/.

Fish, R., & Conant, J. E. (1976). *Every member evangelism for today*. New York: Harper & Row Publishers.

Foster, R. J. (1978). *Celebration of discipline*. San Francisco: Harper-Collins Publishers.

Frazee, R. (2001). *The connecting church*. Grand Rapids: Zondervan Publishing House. Freeman, C. (2011). *Holy bones, holy dust: How relics shaped the history of medieval Europe*. New Haven: Yale University Press.

Frost, M., & Hirsch, A. (2003). *The shaping of things to come: Innovation and mission for the 21st-century church*. Peabody: MA: Hendrickson Publishers.

Fulton, B. (2015). *China's urban Christians: A light that cannot be hidden*. Eugene, OR: Pickwick Publications.

Garrett, J. L., Jr. (1995). *Systematic theology* (Vol. 2). Grand Rapids: William B. Eerdmans Publishing Company.

Garrison, D. (2004). *Church planting movements: How God is redeeming a lost world*. Richmond: WIGTake Resources.

George, S. (2003). Terror-culture: Worth living for or worth dying for. In R. Tiplady (Ed.), *One world or many? The impact of globalization on mission* (pp. 5570). Pasadena: William Carey Library.

Gibbs, E., & Bolger, R. K. (2005). *Emerging churches*. Grand Rapids: Baker Academic.

Gombis, T. G. (2010). *The drama of Ephesians: Participating in the triumph of God*. Downers Grove, IL: Inter-Varsity Press.

Gonzalez, J. L. (1970). *A history of Christian thought, Vol. 1: From the beginnings to the council of Chalcecon*. Nashville: Abingdon Press.

Gonzalez, J. L. (1971). *A history of Christian thought, Vol. 2: From Augustine to the eve of the Reformation*. Nashville: Abingdon Press.

Gorman, M. J. (2015). *Becoming the gospel: Paul, participation, and mission*. Grand Rapids: William B. Eerdmans Publishing Company.

Grenz, S. J., & Franke, J. R. (2001). *Beyond foundationalism*. Louisville: Westminster John Knox Press.

Grenz, S. J., & Smith, J. T. (2014). *Created for community: Connecting   Christian belief with Christian living*. Grand Rapids: Baker   Academic.

Guder, D. L. (1998a). Missional connectedness: The community of communities in mission. In D. L. Guder (Ed.), *Missional church: A vision for the sending of the church in North America* (pp. 248-68). Grand Rapids: William B. Eerdmans Publishing Company.

Guder, D. L. (1998b). Missional structures: The particular community. In D. L. Guder (Ed.), *Missional church: A vision for the sending of the church in North America* (pp. 221-47). Grand Rapids: William B. Eerdmans. Publishing Company.

Haah, K. (2014). A beautiful community of diversity: New City Church. In M. L. Branson & N. Warnes (Eds.), *Starting missional churches* (pp. 86-105). Downers Grove, IL: IVP Books.

Hardin, L. T. (2009). *The spirituality of Jesus*. Grand Rapids: Kregel Publications. Harrington, B., & Absalom, A. (2016). *Discipleship that fits*. Grand Rapids: Zondervan Press.

Harrington, B., & Patrick, J. (2017). *The Disciple-maker's handbook*. Grand Rapids: Zondervan Press.

Hays, J. D. (2010). *The message of the prophets: A survey of the prophetic and apocalyptic books of the OldTestament.* Grand Rapids: Zondervan.

Hull, B. (1990). *The disciple-making church.* Grand Rapids: Fleming H. Revell.

Hunsberger, G. R. (1998). Missional vocation: Called and sent to represent the reign of God. In D. L. Guder (Ed.), *Missional church: A vision for the sending of the church in North America* (pp. 77 109). Grand Rapids: William B. Eerdmans.

Hunter, G. G. (1992). *How to reach secular people.* Nashville: Abingdon Press. ION. (2004). *Making disciples of oral learners.* Lima, NY: Elim Publishing.

Jacobsen, E. O. (2003). *Sidewalks in the kingdom.* Grand Rapids: Brazos Press.

Jacobsen, D. (2011). *The world's Christians: Who they are, where they are, and how they got there.* West Sussex, UK: Wiley Blackwell Publications.

Jenkins, P. (2007). *The next Christendom: The coming of global Christianity.* New York: Oxford University Press.

Kimball, D. (2003). *The emerging church.* Grand Rapids: Zondervan Press.

Koehler, P. F. (2010). *Telling God's story with power.* Pasadena: William Carey Library.

Kostenberger, A. J., and O'Brien, P. T. (2001). *Salvation to the ends of the earth: A biblical theology of mission.* Downers Grove, IL: Inter-Varsity Press.

Life Church. (2018). Retrieved January 2, 2018, from https://www.life.church/.

Linthicum, R. C. (1997). Networking: Hope for the church   in the city. In H. M. Conn (Ed.), *Planting and growing urban churches: From dream to reality* (pp. 164-81). Grand Rapids: Baker Books.

Little, D. (2015). *Effective discipling in Muslim   communities.* Downers   Grove, IL: IVP Academic. Longenecker, B. W. (2009). Socio-economic profiling for the first urban Christians. In T. D. Still & D. G. Horrell (Eds.), *After the first urban Christians: The social-scientific study of Pauline Christianity twenty-five years later* (pp. 36-59). New York: T & T Clark International.

Looney, J. (2015). *Crossroads of the nations: Diaspora, globalization, and evangelism.* Portland, OR: Urban   Loft Publishers.

Lynch, J. H. (2010). *Early Christianity.* New York: Oxford University Press.

MacArthur, J. (1991). *Keys to spiritual growth.* Grand Rapids: Fleming H. Revell.

MacKenzie, G. (2017). Crisis and transformation from monocultural to multicultural: The St. Andrew's Scots Presbyterian Church and the Sin Heng Taiwanese Presbyterian Church. In G. Hart, C. R. Little   & J. Wang (Eds.), *Churches on mission: God's grace abounding to the nations* (pp. 137-60). Pasadena: William Carey Library.

MacMillan, N. C. (2014). Creating third spaces: The light @ Bare Bulb Coffee. In M. L. Branson & N. Warnes (Eds.), *Starting missional churches* (pp. 106-19). Downers Grove, IL: IVP Books.

Mahiaini, W. (2003). Globalization: A view from Africa. In R. Tiplady (Ed.), *One world or many? The impact of   globalization on mission* (pp. 155-66). Pasadena: William Carey Library.

Malone, K. (2006). *Hearing Christ's voice*. Garland, TX: Hannibal Books.

Malone, K. (2009). *The sword of the Spirit*. Smyrna, DE: Missional Press.

Malone, K. (2016a). *City church: Working together to transform cities*. Skyforest, CA: Urban Loft Publishers.

Malone, K. (2016b). Rural migration and the development of urban cultures in the United States. *International Journal of Urban Transformation, 1*, 71-94.

Malone, K. (2018). Peter's evangelistic preaching in Acts 2:14-38. Unpublished presentation from Future Leadership Foundation Consultation with the El Salvador Baptist Association. San Salvador.

Martin, D. B. (2009). Patterns of belief and patterns of life: Correlations in *The first urban Christians* and since. In T. D. Still & D. G. Horrell (Eds.), *After the first urban Christians: The social scientific study of Pauline Christianity twenty-five years later* (pp. 116-33). New York: T & T Clark International.

Marty, M. (2009). *The Christian world*. New York: Modern Library.

Mayers, M. K. (1974). *Christianity confronts culture*. Grand Rapids: Zondervan Press.

McCallum, D., & Lowery, J. (2006). *Organic disciplemaking*. Houston: Touch Publications.

McGowan, A. B. (2014). *Ancient Christian worship*. Grand Rapids: Baker Academic.

McGrath, A. E. (2013). *Christian history*. West Sussex, UK: Wiley Blackwell Publishing.

McMahan, A. (2012). The strategic nature of urban ministry. In G. Fujino, T. R. Sisk & T. C. Casino (Eds.), *Reaching the city: Reflections on urban mission for the twenty-first century* (pp. 1-17). Pasadena: William Carey Library.

McNeal, R. (2003). *The present future: Six tough questions for the church.* San Francisco: Jossey-Bass.

Mcquarrie, M., Fernandes, N., & Shepard, C. (2013). The field of struggle, the office, and the flat: Protest and aspiration in a Mumbai slum. *Public Culture, 25*(2), 315-48.

McRaney, W. (2003). *The art of personal evangelism.* Nashville: B & H Academic.

Meachum, J. (2007). *American gospel: God, the founding fathers, and the making of a nation.* New York: Random House Publishing.

Meeks, W. A. (1983). *The first urban Christians: The social world of the apostle Paul.* New Haven: Yale University Press.

Moody, D. (1991). Baptism in theology and practice. In P. Basden & D. S. Dockery (Eds.), *The people of God: Essays on the believers' church* (pp. 41-50). Nashville: Broadman Press.

Morgenthaler, S. (1995). *Worship evangelism.* Grand Rapids: Zondervan.

Mullin, R. B. (2008). *A short world history of Christianity.* Louisville: Westminster John Knox Press.

Neumann, M. (1999). *Home groups for urban cultures.* Pasadena: William Carey Library.

O'Brien, B. J. (2010). *The strategically small church.* Minneapolis: Bethany House.

Ott, C., & Wilson, G. (2011). *Global church planting.* Grand Rapids: Baker Academic.

Parr, S. R. (2010). *Sunday school that really works.* Grand Rapids: Kregel Publications.

Perkins, J. (1982). *With justice for all.* Ventura, CA: Regal Books.

Peterson, E. H. (2008). *Tell it slant.* Grand Rapids: William B. Eerdmans Publishing Company.

Pierson, P. E. (2009). *The dynamics of Christian mission: History through a missiological perspective.* Pasadena: William Carey International University Press.

Pippert, R. M. (1979). *Out of the salt-shaker & into the world.* Downers Grove, IL: Inter-Varsity Press.

Raley, M. (2009). *The diversity culture.* Grand Rapids: Kregel Publications.

Reno, R. R. (2002). Postmodern irony and Petronian Humanism: The new challenges of evangelism. In C. E. Braaten & R. W. Jenson (Eds.), *The strange new world of the gospel* (pp. 55-72). Grand Rapids: William B. Eerdmans Publishing Company.

Robinson, M., & Smith, D. (2003). *Invading secular space.* London: Monarch Books.

Roof, W. C.. (1999). *Spiritual marketplace: Baby boomers and the remaking of American religion.* Princeton: Princeton University Press.

Roxburgh, A. J. (2011). *Missional: Joining God in the neighborhood.* Grand Rapids: Baker Books.

Saliers, D. E. (1994). *Worship as theology.* Nashville: Abingdon Press.

Sanneh, L. (2008). *Disciples of all nations: Pillars of world Christianity*. New York: Oxford University Press.

Sassen, S. (2013). Does the city have speech? *Public Culture, 25*(2), 209-21.

Scanlon, A. C. (1984). Planning A holistic strategy for urban witness. In L. L. Rose & C. K. Hadaway (Eds.), *An urban world: Churches face the future* (pp. 167 88). Nashville: Broadman Press.

Seel, D. J. (2018). *The new Copernicans*. Nashville: Thomas Nelson Publishers.

Shaw, M. (2010). *Global awakening: How 20th-Century revivals triggered a Christian revolution*. Downers Grove, IL: IVP Academic.

Shaw, R. (2014). *Spiritual equipping for mission*. Downers Grove, IL: IVP Books.

Simson, W. (1999). *Houses that change the world*. Carlisle, Cumbria, UK: OM Publishing.

Slaughter, M., & Bird, W. (2002). *Unlearning church*. Loveland, CO: Group Publishing.

Smith, B. (2008). *City signals: Principles and practices for ministering in today's global communities* Birmingham, AL: New Hope Publishers.

Snyder, H. A. (1975). *The problem of wineskins*. Downers Grove, IL: Inter-Varsity Press.

Snyder, H. A. (1977). *Community of the king*. Downers Grove, IL: Inter Varsity Press.

Snyder, H. A. (1996). *Radical renewal: The problem with wineskins today*. Houston: Touch Publications.

Snyder, H. A. (2016). *Small voice, big city: The challenge of urban mission*. Skyforest, CA: Urban Loft Publishers.

Snyder, H. A., & Runyon, D. V. (2002). *Decoding the church*. Grand Rapids: Baker Books.

Sparks, P., Soerens, T., & Friesen, D. J. (2014). *The new parish: How neighborhood churches are transforming mission, discipleship and community*. Downers Grove, IL: Inter-Varsity Press.

Stanley, P. D., & Clinton, J. R. (1992). *Connecting: The mentoring relationships you need to succeed in life*. Colorado Springs: Nav Press.

Stark, R. (1997). *The rise of Christianity: How the obscure, marginal Jesus movement became the dominant religious force in the Western World in a few centuries*. San Francisco: Harper Collins Publishers.

Stark, R. (2003). *For the glory of God: How monotheism led to reformations, science, witch-hunts, and the end of slavery*. Princeton: Princeton University Press.

Stark, R., & Wang, X. (2015). *A star in the East: The rise of Christianity in China*. West Conshohocken, PA: Templeton Press.

Stetzer, E. (2014). Multisite churches are here, and here, and here to stay. Retrieved January 2, 2018, from http://www.christianitytoday.com/edstetzer/2014/febr ary/multisite-churches-are-here-to-stay.

Stetzer, E., & Rainer, T. S. (2010). *Transformational church*. Nashville: B & H Books.

Stroope, M. W. (2017). *Transcending mission: The eclipse of a modern tradition*. Downers Grove, IL: IVP Academic.

Swartz, D. (1990). *The magnificent obsession*. Colorado Springs: Nav-Press.The Village Church. (2018). Retrieved January 2, 2018 from http://multiply.thevillagechurch.net/.

Thompson, W. O. (1981). *Concentric circles of concern*. Nashville: Broadman Press.

Thrasher, B. (2003). *A journey to victorious praying*. Chicago: Moody Press.

Tokyo Baptist Church. (2018). Retrieved June 22, 2018, from http://tokyobaptist.org/.

Top 20 megacities by population. Retrieved July 25, 2017, from https://www.allianz.com/en/about_us/open knowledge/topics/demography/articles/150316-top-20 megacities-by-population.html/#!m4432cf0e-cb70 4ff1-bc0e 5e5c2797e856.

Turner, P. (2002). The powerless of talking heads: Re evangelization in the postmodern world—the place of ethics. In C. E. Braaten & R. W. Jenson (Eds.), *The strange new world of the gospel* (pp. 73 93). Grand Rapids: William B. Eerdmans Publishing Company.

Van Gelder, C. (1998). Missional context: Understanding North American culture. In D. L. Guder (Ed.), *Missional church: A vision for the sending of the church in North America* (pp. 18 45). Grand Rapids: William B. Eerdmans Publishing Company.

Warnes, N. (2014). Growing roots in a secularized context. In M. L. Branson & N. Warnes (Eds.), *Starting missional churches* (pp. 120 39). Downers Grove, IL: IVP Books.

Webber, R. (1998). *Planning blended worship*. Nashville: Abingdon Press.

Wellborn, L. L. (2016). Inequality in Roman Corinth: Evidence from diverse sources evaluated by a Neo Recardian Model. In J. R. Harrison and L. L. Wellborn (Eds.), *The first urban churches 2: Roman Corinth* (pp. 47-84). Atlanta: SBL Press.

White, J. F. (2000). *Introduction to Christian worship.* Nashville: Abingdon Press.

Wilson, F. (2003). Globalization from a grassroots, two thirds world perspective: A snapshot. In R. Tiplady(Ed.), *One world or many? The impact of globalization on mission* (pp. 167-88). Pasadena: William Carey Library.

Wright, C. J. H. (2006). *The mission of God: Unlocking the Bible's grand narrative.* Downers Grove, IL: IVP   Academic.

Wright, C. J. H. (2010). *The mission of God's people: A biblical theology of the church's mission.* Grand Rapids: Zondervan.

Xu, Z. (2017). A tale of three urban churches: The local churches' role of mission in contemporary China. In G. Hart, C. R. Little & J. Wang (Eds.), *Churches on mission: God's grace abounding to the nations* (pp. 115-36). Pasadena: William Carey Library.

CPSIA information can be obtained
at www.ICGtesting.com
Printed in the USA
LVHW021023111119
636959LV00005B/1963